Praise for *Family Champions and Champion Families*

"Joshua and Greg have unearthed a gem — the most effective family leaders don't always have business cards or even formal authority. Their work has encouraged and challenged me to identify and celebrate the 'nontraditional' leaders and influencers in my own family."

—Chris Herschend
Vice Chair, Herschend Enterprises

"I hope that those who read this book will recognize the importance of the family champion role, and how they seek to unify and help the multigenerational family business. I'll recommend this book especially to executives in family business, as the work of the family champion is focused on positively and directly improving trust amongst all three spheres of family business by actively promoting clarity of mission, values, communication, professional boundaries and healthy development of governance processes. As the family develops into a champion family, business leaders breathe a sigh of relief and outside directors and non-family employees see and feel a more certain sense of stability and commitment by the family."

—Heidi Vermeer-Quist, Psy.D.
Psychologist (Clinical & Family Business Consulting)
G3, Former Ownership Council Chair, and Former
Board Member of Vermeer Corporation

Family Champions
and
Champion Families

Written by advisors from The Family Business Consulting Group, our collection of family business books provides useful information on a broad range of topics that concern the family business enterprise, including succession planning, board building, family leadership, retirement planning, and more. The books are written by experts who have consulted with thousands of enterprising families the world over, giving the reader practical, effective, and time-tested insights to everyone involved in family business.

THE
FAMILY BUSINESS
CONSULTING GROUP

The Family Business Consulting Group, Inc., founded in 1994, is the leading business consultancy exclusively devoted to helping family enterprises prosper across generations.

THE FAMILY BUSINESS LEADERSHIP SERIES

This series of books is comprised of concise guides and thoughtful compendiums to the most pressing issues that anyone involved in a family firm may face. Each volume covers a different topic area and provides the answers to some of the most common and challenging questions.

Titles include:

Family Business Governance: Maximizing Family and Business Potential

Siblings and the Family Business: Making it work for Business, the Family, and the Future

Family Business Succession: The Final Test of Greatness

Innovation in the Family Business: Succeeding Through Generations

Family Meetings: How to Build a Stronger Family and a Stronger Business, 2nd ed.

How Families Work Together

Developing Family Business Policies: Your Guide to the Future

Family Business Ownership: How to be an Effective Shareholder

Letting Go: Preparing Yourself to Relinquish Control of the Family Business

The Family Constitution: Agreements to Secure and Perpetuate Your Family and Your Business

Effective Leadership in the Family Business

From Siblings to Cousins: Prospering in the Third Generation and Beyond

Family Education for Business-Owning Families: Strengthening Bonds by Learning Together

All of the books were written by members of The Family Business Consulting Group and are based on both our experiences with thousands of client families as well as our empirical research at leading research universities the world over. Available from Palgrave Macmillan and Amazon.

Family Champions
and
Champion Families

Developing Family Leaders to
Sustain the Family Enterprise

Joshua Nacht and Greg Greenleaf

Family Champions and Champion Families:
Developing Family Leaders to Sustain the Family Enterprise
by Joshua Nacht and Greg Greenleaf

Copyright © 2018 by
The Family Business Consulting Group, Inc.

Printed in the United States of America

First Printing, 2018

ISBN: 978-0692162804

The Family Business Consulting Group, Inc.
8770 West Bryn Mawr Avenue, Suite 1340
Chicago, Illinois 60631

www.thefbcg.com

This book is dedicated to the memory of Leonard and Susan Nacht, who always inspired people to be their best. It is also dedicated to all current and future family champions. May your work find great success and help you foster your own champion families.

Joshua Nacht

This book is dedicated to my wife Rebecca, who is my family's champion and to all the champion families whom I have had the honor to work with and learn from.

Gregory Greenleaf

CONTENTS

FIGURES

PREFACE

Why we wrote this book

Josh became intrigued by the idea of the family champion while interviewing members of large, multigenerational family firms as part of the Good Fortune independent research project initiated by family business professor/consultant Dennis Jaffe. The study, which involved more than 40 families, focused on the factors that have helped family firms endure longer than 100 years. In multiple interviews, Josh found he was talking to the same type of person: a family owner who was not employed by the business but exerted large leadership influence on family members and the broader enterprise. These family owners often held official titles, such as family council chair, and their influence was both formal and informal. In many cases, they ultimately devoted themselves full-time to ownership and related issues, sometimes in compensated positions.

These people played a key role in helping the family come together and develop their capabilities (individually and as a group) as owners of a complex family enterprise. Josh came to think of them as *family champions* and noticed that they shared some core characteristics. These people were:

- Energetic, self-motivated, skilled at communication
- Committed to duty and responsibility toward their family legacy
- Trusted by the family
- Operating from a position of informal power
- Actively involved in governance as owners, though not working in the business

In general, family champions acted as *catalysts*. In order to facilitate significant development and change throughout the family, they engaged and inspired the family to work collectively to sustain their legacy.

The family champion concept fascinated Josh in part because the main focus of leadership for next-generation family enterprises (for families, family business advisors, and researchers) has been on who will lead the *business*, given its impact on the family's financial health, reputation, and other dimensions. But as business families grow in size and complexity, the importance of the *ownership group* grows concurrently. The *family* leaders occupy an ever-increasing role in helping the family to be active, engaged, and contributing owners and stewards—just as many of Josh's research interviewees did. Strong family leaders promoted knowledge and capability among owners that contributed strongly to business success and family harmony. In fact, with respect to the success of the entire family business system, Josh came to believe leadership of the owners is *as important* as leadership of the business.

In line with this thinking, he became deeply interested in the origins, characteristics, influence pathways, development, and effects of family champions, along with the dynamics of their collective counterpart, the champion family. That interest became the foundation for his doctoral research topic: the role of the family champion. Josh shared his research interests with a broad range of people affiliated with family businesses, including his own, and they often responded, "I know exactly what you're talking about—you need to talk to *this* person." People recognized the role, but lacked the language to talk about it. With affirmed interest in the topic, he completed a robust study including interviews with 14 people who saw themselves as functioning in the family champion role. The Family Firm Institute recognized Josh's research as Best Doctoral Dissertation in 2016, and he's eager to share what he learned with a broader audience.

As Josh was completing his research and moving into a family consulting role, Greg was continuing his own work as a trusted advisor to diverse family businesses. Greg has advised families for more than 15 years, building on his background as a family therapist and president of one of his family's businesses. This unique background helped him to identify the complex group-level challenges business families face, and to shape thoughtful strategies for overcoming them while building family bonds.

Over time, Greg began to see that some business families were much more adept than others at anticipating and addressing multi-dimensional problems. These families proactively created conflict-resolution systems, for example, along with building advisory and fiduciary boards and promoting strong, open communication channels. Greg saw that these families usually included one or more members who helped unite them in facing such complex challenges as transitioning from one generation to the next and developing strong governance measures. Greg sought out these prospective family champions individually and encouraged each one to take on a leadership role, providing them with guidance and mentorship.

Additionally, Greg thought of such effective families as belonging to a special category within family business and, upon hearing about Josh's research, began to think of them as *champion families*, the collective version of the family champion. Based on the families we and our colleagues have advised and observed over many years, we refined the family champion and champion family concepts together.

What's in this book

The structure of this book is simple, accessible, and easy to understand.

- Chapter 1: Introduction to the concepts of family champions and champion families, in the context of the multigenerational family business and the 3-Circle Model.
- Chapters 2 and 3: Finer focus on the family champion and champion family concepts: How do they originate, what are their characteristics, and what topics should you keep in mind for each?
- Chapters 4 and 5: How to identify and foster family champions and champion family qualities. Clear examples and practical tips that show how family champions create champion families.
- Chapter 6: Summary with specific advice on how to start working on championship elements in your family.

Each chapter ends with questions for you to consider, based on the material you've just read, to stimulate your thinking about championship ideas and issues related to your situation.

Who can benefit from this book?

These ideas are applicable to a variety of people. Here are the main groups we had in mind:

- *Multigenerational business families* across many sectors and geographies, grappling with increasingly complex systems and growing families. Especially valuable if you are going through transition, when you might be unsure about succession or leadership and how to best manage your family-ownership group. In such cases, your potential family champions can act in positive and effective ways. But the ideas here are relevant to any multigenerational business family at any point in its development.

- *Champion families* who want to continue to perpetuate their achievements and promote continuity. The work in these families is never done—in line with the concept of *continuous learning*—and the most successful families are always looking for ways to incorporate beneficial, applicable information to promote their longevity.
- *Individuals within family business*, from any of the three circles: family, owner, business employee. This includes older-generation members who want to put the best people and processes in place for the business longer term. It also includes rising-generation members who see transition-related and other challenges and want to make a difference, whether as budding family champions or just as owners seeking positive impact.
- *Professionals who work with or govern family business* and want to understand more fully the dynamics and patterns that influence their performance and the family's well-being. This includes:
  - Non-family executives
  - Family firm HR managers
  - Family business advisors
  - Financial services professionals (bankers, accountants, wealth advisors)
  - Attorneys or educators who specialize in family business (such as professors within family business programs at universities)
  - Independent directors, non-family executives, and trustees

All of these groups can support the efforts of family champions and champion families, working toward shared goals.

INTRODUCTION

Family business

Is it your livelihood? Your legacy? Both? Regardless of your level of involvement, you want the enterprise to succeed and endure. You don't need us to tell you that all businesses need visionary leadership and effective management. But the road to business success can be treacherous, and family businesses often last no more than a generation or two. You—and we—want yours to do better.

Successful businesses often struggle to remain viable against uncertain economic times, technological advances, shifting consumer preferences, and volatile markets—even without the complexity of dealing with family members. And some family businesses manage to flourish through multiple generations despite these challenges. What makes them different? More important, how can you learn from the experiences of what we call champion family businesses?

These successful family businesses take a long view, investing in the company's development for future success. The champion family concept is linked to the family champion, a family owner who acts as a catalyst to help other family members become more effective. This is important to you because:

Family champions create champion families.

Long before we collaborated to write this book, each of us spent years developing professional and personal expertise with family dynamics and family businesses. We have both been involved in our own family businesses, as well as earning academic degrees in relevant subjects. These backgrounds built our interest in successful family champions and champion families. Studying them has enabled us, as consultants, to help many different kinds of family enterprises to achieve their business and family goals.

Our objective

We want this book to stimulate your thoughts and inspire you to appropriate action. You are not alone in facing issues at the intersection of family, business, and ownership. Every family firm is living some version of the 3-Circle Model we present in Chapter 1. Each one must navigate these treacherous waters, and it takes a lot of work. The concepts we present can apply to any multigenerational family firm at any stage of growth.

Although the concept of a champion family overlaps with previous work, the family champion idea is pioneering and based on thoughtful research. Such individuals emerge naturally within a business family and, through their efforts, move the family toward champion family status. That theme reverberates throughout this book.

There is no simple how-to, step-by-step formula to success. So this book is more *inspirational than prescriptive.* Part of what makes business families fascinating is that there are so many different permutations of family business systems, and so many ways that such families engage with their particular situations. We present concepts in a manner designed to stimulate your thinking about tricky challenges in your own situation. Our definitions are purposely open to interpretation so that you can adapt the ideas to your unique conditions. Whatever approach you take, the most important objective is to get the right people and approaches for your system in place, rather than trying to match someone else's, no matter how well it has worked for them.

So we encourage you to see the ideas here through the lens of your own family situation and apply them flexibly, with an emphasis on continuous learning. That's what makes family champions and champion families dynamic and vital. Study the examples we describe and note the approaches and strategies you can apply to your business. The wisdom from these winning families and their stories can guide you around common obstacles and provide inspiration to your business family, regardless of its size or complexity. It is our sincere wish that you use this knowledge to develop your own successful family champions and enduring champion families.

—Joshua Nacht and Greg Greenleaf

CHAPTER 1: OVERVIEW

What are family champions and champion families?

At the beginning, even Sofia was surprised by her enthusiasm for taking on ownership issues related to her family business[1]. The 42-year-old was a fourth-generation member of a nearly century-old manufacturing business based in the southeastern United States. In the 2010s, Sofia was enjoying her career as a technology consultant outside the family firm when her father—the business CEO, now nearing retirement—urged her to become more involved as an owner. Specifically, he wanted her to assist the family council in transferring leadership from the third generation to the fourth.

Sofia knew that rising to her father's request would be no easy task. Her parents' generation had been rigidly patriarchal, with all major business decisions to date made by the men in the family. Sofia's mother and aunts had little influence and almost no say in business matters, and had accepted this situation. Sofia also knew that this type of family business culture would not sit well with her female cousins, many of whom were successful in their own careers and used to calling the shots in their own lives.

With all of this in mind, Sofia agreed to become more involved. Right away, she began to engage the family proactively in a more democratic, consensus-driven

---

[1] The examples here are inspired by real-life examples, but with identifying details changed to preserve confidentiality.

leadership approach to the transition—a big undertaking. Long-standing family dissension threatened their goals on multiple fronts. Aware of the potential danger, Sofia took the initiative to go beyond her father's original request. She made concerted efforts to improve the family's ability to cooperate, from establishing regular meetings to helping the contentious relatives reconcile or at least work together.

Sofia's efforts yielded good results by the time her father retired. The family communicated more effectively and openly on a range of family and business issues, and several cousins stepped up to take greater responsibility on ownership and governance issues. No family member was equipped to lead the business, so they selected a non-family CEO. Although the new executive was well-liked and effective, he also had ambitious growth plans. The family was excited by the vision, but Sofia realized they were not prepared to own a business of the envisioned magnitude, run by a non-family member. Under her leadership, they created a strategic plan to develop their ownership capabilities to steward the business more responsibly and effectively in the long term.

Sofia had come to understand that, regardless of the progress she made in developing her family members as individual and collective owners, new challenges always lay ahead. Luckily, she was excited about taking them on, and she worked to engage the family at large to participate in the process. The family gradually did their share, making a focused effort to gain new skills and perspective to manage complex issues where family and business intersected.

Sofia is a family champion, a family owner who acts as a catalyst, inspiring and assisting fellow members to become more effective owners, with positive results for the family and the business. As this example suggests, family champions and champion families are interlinked concepts. The former helps to create the latter. Family champion Sofia has been the catalyst that helped to transform her family into a champion family.

In later chapters we will return to the example of family champion Sofia and her family—which she helped transform into a champion family—along with other illustrations of individuals and families that exemplify these concepts (and some that don't!). In this first chapter, our focus is on setting the context for topics we discuss later: defining them carefully, understanding why they matter, and pointing out some high-level issues to keep in mind.

The multigenerational family business and the 3-Circle Model[2]

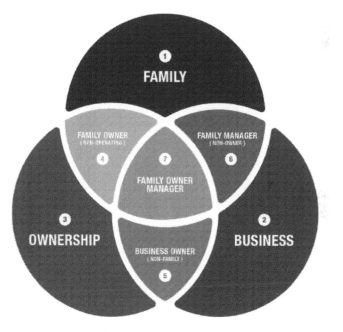

Figure 1: The 3-Circle Model

Family businesses come in all shapes and sizes. The family champion and champion family concepts are relevant to *multigenerational family firms* as these businesses grow

---

[2] 3-Circle Model from Tagiuri, R., & Davis, J. (1996). "Bivalent attributes of a family firm." *Family Business Review*, 9 (2), Summer 1996.

more complex. But, although the concepts originated from larger and more complex multigenerational families, they apply to most business families facing the same challenges. That includes any family with multiple generations working and owning together. These challenges include:

- Several generations as owners (and employees, in some cases)
- Geographically dispersed owners, within and across countries
- Varied levels of ownership and wealth (such as concentration of ownership in more senior generations or smaller family branches)

These characteristics typically signify differences in family members' values, cultural influences, risk appetites, and other factors. That means a high potential for misalignment of interests and goals as related to the business and family. Thus the ideas discussed in this book are particularly applicable to complex family systems with significant diversity on key dimensions.

Like many other family business researchers and advisors, we have found the 3-Circle Model of family business helpful for understanding the challenges inherent in family enterprise. Understanding the family enterprise system is critical to effective family champion and champion family functioning.

As Figure 1 shows, the family business involves three overlapping systems: family, business, and ownership. The family circle, or system, represents the group of people related by blood or marriage to the founding or owning family. The business system includes employees of the firm (family and non-family managers and other employees). The ownership circle includes anyone who owns equity in the family firm, typically family members of multiple generations.

Although this seems simple and logical enough, even a basic understanding of the model suggests that the three systems will likely have conflicting visions and goals. These differences can cause tension within the broader enterprise. For example, when discussing terms for family member employment, the family system might push for more flexible criteria, but the business system might be less accommodating. In addition, a given person might occupy one, none, several, or all of the seven territories represented by the circles and their overlapping regions. Each of those territories involves a different point of view and set of priorities—again leading to potential conflict around vision and goals.

Throughout this book, we return to the 3-Circle Model during discussions of specific issues and challenges that afflict family champions and champion families.

What is a family champion?

As suggested by the example of Sofia presented earlier, at a high level, a family champion is a family owner or leader who acts as a *catalyst* to inspire fellow members to meet their potential as owners and takes active steps to develop the ownership potential of individuals and the family.

As shown in Figure 1, the 3-Circle Model, a family champion is always a family member, usually an owner (which helps boost commitment to managing ownership issues), but usually not an employee (which affords more space to handle ownership issues). Family champions come from a variety of origins, and there is no description that describes them all. They rise to their responsibility through circumstances—as different as they are—most often because there has been a business transition, they have taken an interest through education, a leadership void has occurred, or someone in the family has encouraged them to become leaders. But some common desirable attributes make good family champions:

Commitment to family development. Deeply devoted to developing the ownership group, both collectively and as individuals. This commitment can stem from the champion's background, culture, personality, education, or some combination. A sense of responsibility and purpose motivates the champion to act in the first place, and to continue exerting positive influence on the family through both prosperous and difficult times.

High awareness of family needs and dynamics. They get their families, even if they don't have frequent contact with fellow members. They understand the family's needs, desires, and challenges at a deep level and harness that understanding to benefit the family and the business on multiple levels. This benefit can range from helping the family understand how their values influence (or should influence) the business to mending fences between members, generations, or branches. Family champions are empathetic, even when they do not necessarily agree with other family members' opinions.

Willingness to work as part of a team. A business can have more than one family champion. We know a group of three female family shareholders who have collectively served as family champions for their multigenerational family trucking firm. They have acted as a catalyzing force to address the lack of effective governance in their enterprise (later chapters discuss this example in more detail).

Readiness to speak—and act on—what the family needs. This is the person who stands up—literally or figuratively— and says, "We need to do better as a family. If we want to own this business long term and pass on our family legacy, we have to be the best owners we can be." Family champions are personally motivated to lead this work and recognize that they are uniquely suited to begin it. They don't wait for someone else to do it. They take initiative and begin the change themselves.

Ability—and willingness—to wear many hats. At once a promoter, supporter, and influencer, with a meaningful impact on the ownership group. Roles might include strategist (for business and family), facilitator, educator, mediator, therapist, intermediary, network broker, and many others. Effective family champions recognize which hat to wear when, and are constantly building their skills across areas through formal and informal means.

Multiple skills. Exhibits abilities in many areas, ranging from business knowledge to interpersonal skills. They need not be experts, but they are intuitive about what will work and can quickly develop insights about family dynamics and the family's relationship with the business. They can work with different people and perspectives, adapting their approach and tactics to help the family reach the next level of development. Family champions are also eager to learn new skills and to invest in their own education and development.

Diverse origins. As we discuss in the next chapter, Family Champions, these individuals can emerge through a variety of circumstances. Some families have a development-oriented culture that cultivates family champions. In other cases, family champions rise to address a crisis or gap, such as a sudden leadership transition.

CHAPTER 1

What is a champion family?

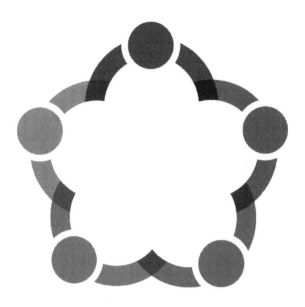

A champion family is a business family that has actively and intentionally invested in its development and thus has created long-term success as a group. It often develops through the efforts of a family champion who stimulates greater commitment, participation, and capability among the broader family. To gain useful insight, we can look at the similarities (shared characteristics) of these champion families. Certain hallmark traits, as well as some observable practical elements, provide guidelines for comparing and evaluating family businesses.

Seven hallmark traits

> These seven traits, or characteristics, appear throughout this book. We explore them in greater depth later to illustrate how example family businesses succeed, how to evaluate yours, and how to identify opportunities for improvement.

Champion families are an inspiration and guide to other business-owning families based on these traits:

1. *Leadership*—that inspires the pursuit of long-term goals and continuous improvement.
2. *Purpose*—shared by family and employees alike, contributing to the success and longevity of the enterprise.
3. *Values*—that characterize the business, determine choices, and guide decisions.
4. *Governance*—by competent, objective, and fair-minded individuals in the best interest of the family and business.
5. *Education*—as an ongoing value and principle, keeping up with social, economic, and technological changes.
6. *Communication*—and transparency throughout both business and family sectors.
7. *Relationships*—based on trust and common interest, willingness to forgive and compromise.

Common elements

The identifying traits of champion families correlate with some observable practical elements:

Track record of progress. A long history of creating the capabilities, structures, insights, and perspective to drive success on both family and business levels. They have weathered the challenges built into family business and constructively created meaningful value of all types across generations.

Forward-looking attitude. Despite past success, a champion family recognizes that they must continue to invest in themselves to sustain their gains and to build their success as a legacy family. There is no resting on their laurels, as tempting as that might be. They have learned that being proactive in their efforts is important and effective for managing their unique challenges and opportunities.

Continuous learning across dimensions. Observable success across key dimensions including financial, relational, and individual, and willing engagement in ongoing learning. The family is ready to advance with the business, rather than being adrift or dissociated. They adopt a philosophy of continual learning and investment in their growth and development. This means devoting time and financial resources to a range of educational initiatives.

Ability to adapt and adopt learning. They do not look to re-invent the wheel. They intentionally learn and adopt what other successful business families have done, applying these experiences to their unique situations. (They read this book!)

Systemic approach. Recognize the need for multiple elements to work in concert, driving family and business success. Develop various ownership-based roles, including compensated positions such as family council chair. Establish or strengthen effective governance structures for the family and the business, with the aim of engaging a range of people. These structures include the family council, business board (including independent directors), task forces, and sub-committees. They make sure these elements are aligned throughout the system to help the family work toward well-defined and shared goals.

Conflict management and prevention. Strong capabilities to manage and even prevent conflicts that occur naturally in the family and business. For example, they learn the dangers of triangulation (talking negatively about someone to others rather than talking to that person directly) and develop healthy ways to address disagreements. They grow from conflict experiences and use these to inform solutions that promote longer-term harmony.

Origination with family champions. They started with the people who took initiative to help the family become effective owners and stewards. Their success happens through consistent and intentional efforts by inspirational figures—it does not occur by accident. Champion families can certainly foster family champions, but there might be less need for a central individual to promote ownership development if the family already does this effectively at the collective level.

We're not the first to propose studying the shared characteristics of successful business families. Our development of the elements of champion families includes some of the thinking offered earlier by our esteemed colleagues in the field of family business. For example, John L. Ward and Randel Carlock advanced the idea of the enterprising family, or one that successfully integrates key aspects of managing the complexities of business and family together for long-term success.[3] They looked specifically at how business families must attend to their values, vision, strategy, investment, and governance at the business and family system levels, arguing that those who do this well— enterprising families—establish a foundation for success over generations.

Similarly, married researchers Isabelle Le Breton-Miller and Danny Miller concluded that successful business families exhibit characteristics including careful commitment of resources (energy, time, and financial capital) and an ethos of ensuring the continuity of family ownership.[4] In their view, families who have endured myriad challenges over time have

---

[3] Carlock, R.S., & Ward, J.L. (2010). *When family businesses are best: The parallel planning process for family harmony and business success.* New York, NY: Palgrave Macmillan US.

[4] Miller, D., & Miller, I.L. (2005). *Managing for the long run: Lessons in competitive advantage from great family businesses.* Boston, MA: Harvard Business School Press.

created continuity, community, connection, and command over challenges as a means to steward the business entity.

Dennis Jaffe's "Good Fortune" research looked into what promoted the success and continuity of 100-year-old business families. He identified a list of key characteristics of enterprising, generative business families including shared purpose and values, continual adaptation, and active development of human capital. The champion-family strengths we've highlighted here align with Jaffe's research findings on long-lasting family enterprises, shown in Figure 2.[5]

We built our ideas on the foundation of others who have studied this field, while extending our thinking to include the concept of the family champion, that individual's role in creating a champion family, and the mutual evolution of both. Our work and past ideas converge on the idea that successful families attend to and improve many different parts of their system over time. In our observation, the seven elements of champion families—which overlap considerably with the ideas proposed by others—are those most central to ongoing success and continuity across the family and business.

With the definitions of family champions and champion families in place, let's turn to why these individuals and groups matter in the broader domain of family enterprise.

[5] Jaffe, D.T. (2013). *Good fortune: Building a hundred year family enterprise.* Milton, MA: Wise Counsel Research.

What 100-year-old family businesses share

1. Shared purpose and values – They don't just focus on money.

2. Family community across generations – They maintain close ties.

3. Professional management of business and financial activities – They know when to seek help from those outside the family.

4. Continual adaptation and resiliency – They are willing to learn and grow.

5. Free choice to remain partners – They choose to work together.

6. Active development of human capital – They work on themselves.

7. Commitment to give back to the community – They support where they're from.

Figure 2: Shared characteristics of 100-year-old family businesses

Why family champions and champion families matter

We think family champions and champion families matter significantly because of the positive impact they make on their stakeholders. Both are aimed at promoting long-term sustainability of the business family, which has an impact not only on the family but on the regional, national, and global economy where the business contributes. By helping the ownership group develop to be the best it can be, champions ensure that this constituency becomes a true asset to the business it owns. Becoming an asset to the business is especially important if the family owns the business, but has no family members working within it.

These non-operating ownership families find themselves in a position of great responsibility, but (possibly unlike previous generations) without a family member leading the business. Champions grow the system by enhancing the capacity of all three circles of the model described earlier—family, business, and ownership. They ensure that the circles are in better alignment and work more effectively together, with less conflict and discord.

We have observed a strong correlation between the family champion's efforts and the performance of the business. In short, the presence of a family champion or champion family boosts business results by ensuring that the family contributes to the success of the business and does not unduly detract from business performance. Fundamentally, the family influences the enterprise through a commitment of resources to the business and genuine dedication to business success. This dedication includes having a non-family member lead the business, in alignment with a pledge to have the best talent at the helm.

For example, Sofia, the family champion from our opening example, was directly responsible for getting high-quality independent directors on her family firm's board. These capable and qualified people would not have agreed to join the board if they had seen evidence that the family was dysfunctional. Any hint of an uncooperative family would have impeded their ability to guide and enhance the business.

Sofia demonstrated to the board candidates that the family was actively engaged in their own work, and were committed to the success of the business. They already recognized the value of independent board members, meaning that the efforts of all parties would be aligned around achieving shared goals. In turn, the board's enhanced effectiveness benefited the business and shareholders. Sofia's family enjoyed many additional benefits from her efforts, including closer bonds, shared vision and goals, and a more genuine interest in working together on family enterprise issues.

In a later chapter we'll meet the Andersons, a Midwest-based third-generation family with businesses in construction and real estate. Like Sofia's family, they display many championship elements, especially at the group level. For example, each generation plays a role in the business, with the founders now in advisory roles, middle generation operating the enterprise, and third generation developing themselves for business and governance roles, with good communication throughout generations and branches. With the help of outside advisors, the family formed a continuity committee to plan ownership and leadership succession, as the second generation looks ahead to move out of operating roles. Alongside that effort, the family has worked to form an advisory board that will evolve into a fiduciary board, along with streamlining operating agreements and updating trusts and estate plans. In this way, this champion family has ensured that ownership acts to complement and advance the business, with mutually beneficial results.

Family champions and champion families are associated with significant benefits for the family enterprise, but until this point there has not been specific information available on how these champions emerge, what qualities they tend to have, and how they can be fostered and supported within the family system. This book fills that informational gap with a central idea that the work of the family champion often helps the business family evolve into a champion family.

CHAPTER 1

Questions to consider

- Why are you interested in the ideas of the family champion and family champions?
- What do you think of the 3-Circle Model? How does it apply to your family and its business? At what intersections in the model do you see challenges for the family?
- What elements of family champions do you see among your family members ... including you?
- What elements of the champion family do you see in your family?
- What are your ideas related to the idea of family championship?
- What are your fears related to family championship?
- What is your highest vision for your business family?

CHAPTER 2: FAMILY CHAMPIONS

The remarkable leadership
of the family champion

The family champion, as defined in Chapter 1, is a family owner or future inheritor who inspires and assists fellow family business members to become more effective owners, with positive benefits for all.

The champion acts as a catalyst and helps develop the ownership family to be the best possible stewards of the enterprise. We've found that the best way to explain the concept is through real-life examples.

This chapter shares examples inspired by successful family champions we've observed or heard about from colleagues, and then it expands the discussion to the origins and function of family champions. Note the broad range of champions, even in this small sample: from those whose families still run the legacy business to those whose families have sold the company and now participate in a family office. In the family office situation, the family jointly manages collective assets (which might include a portfolio of operating businesses and investments), and is commonly thought of as the new family business! We refer to these examples throughout the book.

Family champion examples

All of these people have served as exemplary family champions, driving significant positive change for their families and the businesses they own.

Sofia the Strategist: We first met Sofia in Chapter 1. The 42-year-old, fourth-generation member of a long-standing manufacturing business in the southeastern US, Sofia exerted deep influence on her family, beginning when her father prepared to pass the CEO role to a non-family executive. Sofia recognized the need to replace the system's outdated, patriarchal decision-making process with a more inclusive approach to ownership issues. "Everyone cared about each other and the business," Sofia said, "but there was no system for making decisions as owners, and that resulted in some conflict." She took a strategic approach, guiding fellow owners toward agreement, keeping everyone informed, and generally embracing an interactive role as a hub within the ownership group.

In assuming this role, Sofia achieved the benefits that can result from a high degree of personal investment in championship work and underscored the importance of broad family support for the champion. Thanks largely to her efforts, Sofia's family-enterprise system today is highly advanced. Its functional governance bodies work in concert for the benefit of both family and business. In short, as a family champion, Sofia's capability and increased commitment to tackling complex ownership issues helped develop her family into a genuine champion family.

Lawrence the Listener: Lawrence is a member of a large sixth-generation family, originally from the US East Coast, but now spread across the country. The family's core business was in glass production, but they sold their operating companies over the years, and now manage collective assets together through a family office. The sheer number and geographic dispersion of their 250+ owners led to widely divergent ownership goals and interests. Although the family had recognized the importance of a well-established board of directors and family council, communication between the family office and shareholders had frayed. It tended to flow in only one direction—from the office to owners. Despite their solid governance structure, communication had broken down. The family office made presentations but invited or promoted little true interaction. The office became increasingly concerned that family members wanted to sell shares.

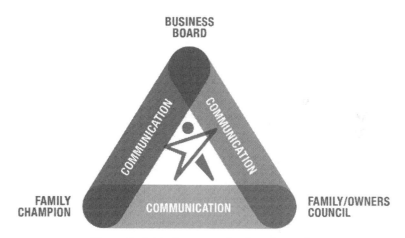

Figure 3: Critical communication channels

Upon election to the family council, Lawrence initiated and led a new process of communication: simply asking questions and listening to family members about what they wanted. This straightforward approach helped Lawrence— and through him, the office—understand that 90% of owners were actually happy with their situation and didn't want to sell. "What they really wanted," Lawrence said, "was to be listened to, and to have their concerns addressed." Lawrence initiated a program in which three family council members met with other shareholders and the business board, asked good questions, and listened to their responses. By listening and opening up communication throughout the governance structure, Lawrence revolutionized how the family council and family interacted, with immediately noticeable results.

The family felt respected and valued, and began to re-engage as shareholders. For example, owners began to provide input, attend office events, show interest, and ask questions, promoting a much more interactive, dynamic relationship between them and the family office. Lawrence's efforts helped create a strong foundation for transforming his extended family into a champion family.

Barry the Builder: Barry grew up in his family business in the Pacific Northwest. The business started in timber, evolved to beverage distribution, and now consists of a large and diversified portfolio of assets and investments. A member of the third generation, Barry had worked his way up from stock boy to CEO. In that role he realized his passion was less about running a business and more about building a family legacy. "What really fired me up was building a business that had a greater purpose beyond profits," Barry said. "I saw there was a path here for me to be able to influence the health of the family and my contribution to it." When a fantastic opportunity emerged, the family chose to sell the business, resulting in a major liquidity event. Barry saw that the family would need greatly increased structure and organization to manage themselves as a group, especially now that they were no longer oriented around the legacy business. Barry took this opportunity to adapt his leadership scope to developing the family.

In the post-sale era, the family remained connected by formal trusts and collective assets, but had no mechanisms for how to work and relate together as owners. So Barry set about to build processes and structures that suited the family's needs. His brother Patrick had tried to do the same earlier but had failed because, unlike Barry, he didn't sufficiently understand how to work within the family's culture. As Barry's uncle noted, "Barry understands the importance of a common vision and what we need to do to keep ourselves connected and develop personal relationships." Barry's efforts helped the family on several fronts, including enhancing their financial knowledge and providing multiple opportunities for collective communication and decision-making throughout the year.

Carla the Coach: Carla is the youngest third-generation member of her family, which owns multiple businesses on the West Coast. Carla's grandfather had emigrated from Brazil to the US several decades earlier, and started a business in industrial steel fabrication. His children, including Carla's parents, diversified the company into real estate development, and the family owned extensive assets in multiple states. As her parents' generation neared retirement, Carla, who had worked as a financial professional outside the family firm, watched as multiple extended family members retained lawyers and began to build coalitions to engage in a destructive power struggle. "Something had to be done," Carla said. "It seemed like the beginning of the end."

Because one of her fellow family members was focused on running the business, Carla attended to fixing governance issues. The all-family board was characterized by poor dynamics and self-dealing. She also worked on the family's interpersonal dynamics and communication patterns, urged members to respect everyone's viewpoint, and avoided taking sides or painting other family members as the bad guys. For example, she helped one cousin understand how his blunt language—including words like *idiot* and *moron*—offended family members and disrupted his message. She convinced him to improve his communication.

As her work gained momentum, trust in her role grew, and Carla worked with the family as a team to develop a common direction and vision. She used the example of sailors navigating by the stars to stay on course. "What's the highest ideal we can aim for as a family?" she asked in various forms and forums. She incorporated members' answers to help create the family's True North Story, the highest aspirational goal of long-term business ownership, as supported by high-quality relationships. In this way, Carla guided family members to work in the same direction, in synch, toward their destination. Development of a clear, collective vision is part of a business family's evolution toward becoming a champion family, and individual family champions often guide their families to work on such visions.

The Thompson Trucking Cousins: Our last example is not an individual family champion, but a group of three third-generation cousins who've worked together to drive important changes for their family ownership group. The Thompsons own a medium-sized trucking company based in a US Mid-Atlantic state, with a long history in the community. The business had grown under the leadership of previous generations. But their challenges included lower-than-ideal reinvestment, a family-member-heavy board that acted merely as a rubber stamp for executive decisions, and an unwritten policy that family members could easily gain employment or board membership in the firm.

The three family champions did not work in the business but recognized its challenges, including the trend for family members to accept dividend checks without any interest in broader enterprise issues. The issues came to a head when a third-generation family employee's substance-abuse problems interfered with his work performance but he refused to take responsibility. The champions worked together to approach the problem strategically, first trying to work with the individual in question (no luck) and then to work with the board. "We tried what we saw as the least disruptive approaches first," one of the cousins said. When the board showed no interest in resolving the issue, the cousin champions rallied fellow owners who'd been uninvolved in the business or board to date, to make changes including professionalizing the board with independent members. "We told our family that we had to change things in the short term to benefit longer term," another champion cousin said.

Under pressure resulting from these developments, the problematic family employee eventually left the business. Several board members stepped down, leaving the board with a majority of independent members. The three cousins made additional improvements, including a healthier distribution policy and the suggestion that the board help management focus on growth opportunities. They instituted formal programs to help develop fourth-generation members interested in employment or governance roles within the enterprise. The Thompson Trucking cousins shared the family champion role and set the right course for their extended family, with plenty of important work still left to do.

What makes a family champion?

As these examples suggest, family champions represent many types of people and modes of influence. They also hail from different families (size, culture, involvement in business operations), business sectors, and geographies. But they share several key elements. We covered some qualities of family champions in Chapter 1. Here we elaborate on those, tying in the family champion examples presented as well as others. Remember that these characteristics of family champions are instrumental in helping them move their families toward becoming champion families.

Figure 4: Characteristics of family champions

Sense of purpose. Family champions feel a strong responsibility to perpetuate their family legacy. This feeling lends a sense of purpose and meaning to their work. The result is an enduring commitment to the success of business *and* family. Intent on positive impact, they take initiative to drive the development of their family as owners—often a large volume of work that must be sustained over years, as suggested by the examples. Family champions typically see themselves as responsible stewards of their family legacy. In their words:

"My commitment is to the family and to the legacy."

"I just found something I love to do, something that drives me and inspires me."

"I realized that no one else was going to do the work of building the family, so I knew I had to."

Thus family champions usually see their work as a *calling*, one that often turns into a more formal role or job within the family enterprise. Barry the Builder exemplifies this element of family championship, as suggested by his quotes about building a business with a "greater purpose for the health of the entire family."

Navigating family dynamics. Family champions are skillful at managing family dynamics at both the interpersonal and cross-generational levels. They appreciate the range of viewpoints, values, and cultural perspectives that appear in multigenerational families based on members' personalities, backgrounds (including early experience, socioeconomic status, and others), and areas of residence. Using their understanding, they work to bridge generations and strive to help the family see diverse perspectives as a collective strength.

Family champions can also play an active role to reconcile family dynamic issues that might be holding the family back. Sometimes a person from a younger generation, for example, can step in and say, "We can't keep repeating the patterns of the past. We need to create a new path forward with new relationships," as Sofia the Strategist did. Family champions might also recognize the need to bring in professionals to help the family improve communications and decision-making. In one other family we know, the family champion actively worked to make sure her generation didn't inherit the negative patterns, including jealousy and conflict, from their parents' generation.

Credibility and trust. Family champions build credibility and trust through their actions and alignment with family culture and values. They are not anointed. Family champions earn the role and position through *authenticity*. People see them as genuinely committed to improving the ownership group—rather than having a self-serving agenda—and able to do it. As they build trust and credibility, champions are better able to engage with the family. A beneficial feedback cycle promotes additional trust in their functions.

Figure 5: Building trust and credibility

Knowledge. Family champions operate at the intersection of family and business. Although some degree of business acumen boosts their legitimacy, it's not required for success. For example, Carla the Coach used her financial knowledge to help her family better understand key business issues as owners. Many family champions end up in dual governance roles—both chair of the family council and director on the business's board, representing the family's voice. For both positions, business ability helps them understand and translate the interconnected elements of business and family.

For this reason, many family champions (regardless of background) seek to bolster their understanding of the business and its financials in order to better lead the ownership group.

Experience. There's no specific training for the family champion role. It requires multiple abilities, experiences, and skills. Some of the most effective champions have widely diverse experiences they can draw upon. Lawrence was a restaurant-owner before becoming his family's champion. Others have worked as teachers or project managers or school board leaders.

Of course, having some business-related experience can be useful in the context of any family business role, but it's not required for championship. That's because champions are able to adapt and integrate their experiences into the new role and use their accumulated proficiencies to their advantage. Additionally, these people invest in their continuous development through a desire to learn more about how to be effective. They invest in leadership development, education about family-business, conferences, peer groups, and other resources that enhance their personal development, for the benefit of the broader family.

Interpersonal skills. Family ownership groups tend to be democratic and non-hierarchical, thus seeking consensus of some form in decision-making. Effective leadership in these situations requires adept listening and communication skills to bridge gaps and identify shared goals. The family champion needs to communicate in a respectful manner with a range of family members and—most important—to listen.

"Lawrence is an excellent listener," several of his cousins agreed. "His ability to help people feel heard has been critical to his success getting us to communicate with each other better." Champions use their interpersonal skills and understanding of family dynamics to model and facilitate healthy interactions. They use these skills to broker solutions throughout the family, building trust, engagement, and commitment.

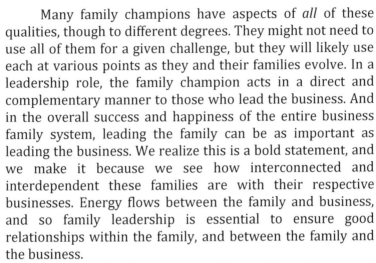

Many family champions have aspects of *all* of these qualities, though to different degrees. They might not need to use all of them for a given challenge, but they will likely use each at various points as they and their families evolve. In a leadership role, the family champion acts in a direct and complementary manner to those who lead the business. And in the overall success and happiness of the entire business family system, leading the family can be as important as leading the business. We realize this is a bold statement, and we make it because we see how interconnected and interdependent these families are with their respective businesses. Energy flows between the family and business, and so family leadership is essential to ensure good relationships within the family, and between the family and the business.

Not every family member is able to achieve this trusted role. As we saw in the case of Barry the Builder, his brother did not understand how to work within the family culture and was unable to be a champion. In another family, a sibling who lived extravagantly failed to take on the champion role because the family didn't see him as aligned with their cultural values. In other cases, a would-be champion might be regarded as genuine, but lack of family support for change prevents the development of that person into a full champion.

Where do family champions come from?

There is no single source or set of circumstances that produces family champions, but we have observed that they are likely to appear in response to a mounting *need* for their service and leadership. In many cases, the need has remained unmet for a long time, perhaps years. The lack of leadership has significant consequences for the family. Some champions describe this situation as "a ship without a rudder." The family feels adrift, without direction. Although it might be tolerable for a short time, this condition robs the family enterprise of the cohesion and alignment it needs for long-term harmony and success.

Champions emerge in these situations when they realize that, with proper direction and guidance, the family could manage and prevent the challenges they face. But family champions usually don't appear overnight. They might consider the role for some time before they commit to it. Many experience a *shift*, or tipping point, that causes them to take on increased engagement and relevance. After this *a-ha* moment, momentum swings in favor of engagement. These shifts happen in many forms and are often interconnected, but they all motivate an inspired person to step up and seek greater capability and impact. In many cases, family champions do not set out to be leaders. They begin by trying to make a *difference* and, through their efforts and engagement, they earn leadership.

Next we present examples of the common, interrelated types of shifts that can motivate future family champions to accept their roles. Although some are more dramatic or time-limited (death, succession, disagreement), they can also represent a slow decline of leadership among ownership. The *no-rudder* situation is an example of slow leadership decline. Sudden shifts, rather than creating a unsustainable situations in and of themselves, usually reveal long-standing issues among owners.

Transition. Business families encounter all sorts of transitions: a key member retires, the business is sold, a matriarch dies. A transition might happen in just part of the system (such as within a family branch), or it might happen throughout. In either case, the shift and turmoil a transition creates can highlight a lack of leadership in the family. The lack of leadership prevents the family from dealing with the challenge effectively. One family champion noted, "It's really interesting how circumstances define leadership. I probably wouldn't have entered our family-business if my uncle and grandfather were still there [both had passed]. So it was their absence that really brought out my leadership ability, which might not have shown up in a more stable situation."

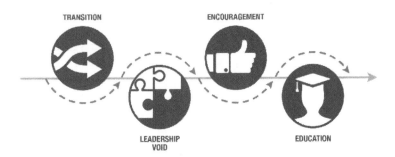

Figure 6: Motivating shifts for family champions

Just as transitions are rarely single events, the emergence of the family leader usually happens over time, and might not coincide with the transition. It might happen later, in response to the ripples caused by the transition. Lawrence, from our earlier example, emerged as a family champion later in his family's evolution. It happened when he joined the family council and saw the growing disconnect between the family office and the ownership group.

Leadership Void. A lack of leadership often motivates the emergence of the family champion, as it did with Lawrence. In some business families, the size and complexity of the family-ownership group grows without evolution of accompanying leadership, whether the result of poor planning, insufficient governance structure or process, ill-fitting leadership for the family, or simple inertia. In many cases, so much attention goes toward who will be leading the *business* that the subject of leadership for the family owners is overlooked and undervalued. Without proper leadership in place, families then find themselves less able to deal with the growing complexity. It's cyclical: a lack of leadership creates ongoing issues that make the absence of leadership more challenging, resulting in even larger issues.

While the business sails full steam ahead, the business leader can do only so much within the family. This is especially true when the business has a non-family CEO whose job does not include (even implicitly) managing the family. The growing void calls some family champions to action. "There was a vacuum and I had the opportunity to step into it," one said. "If I don't do it, who will?" Thus a leadership vacuum is often what motivates a family champion to take charge, as in the example of the Thompson Trucking Cousins, who took action to address their board's lack of strong leadership.

Encouragement. Encouragement represents another potential source of shift for family champions, whether in combination with the example scenarios or on its own. The encouragement can be from another family member (often an older-generation member), trusted advisor, non-family executive, or independent director—anyone with significant influence in the family enterprise. It takes the form of a suggestion to step into an owner-leader role. "You'd be good at serving on the family council," the encourager might say. "Have you considered it?"

The encouragement amounts to an invitation for potential champions to be more involved, to apply their existing or evolving skills to a new role for the family. The encouragement to accept more responsibility is an opportunity, and the family champion must then take advantage of it. Lawrence the Listener's uncle, for example, saw Lawrence's potential and wanted to bring his talents and energy into the family council.

In many cases, senior family members see the need for family-owner leadership, but cannot take on this role themselves because they are focused on running the business. One family champion said, "With the family getting larger and more issues arising, the CEO was becoming distracted from adding shareholder value. So he tapped me on the shoulder one day and said, 'Would you mind taking on something new and different?' At the time, we had nothing set up to involve or engage our shareholders." In this case, the encouragement led to the creation of a family council and the family champion became director of shareholder relations, bridging the family and business and increasing the focus and functioning of both.

Education. In other cases, a shift more *internal* to the champion might be the motivating force. For example, the number of resources for family business education is always increasing. Growing numbers of books, seminars, conferences, webinars, and professional service-providers are dedicated to helping families navigate their landscape. Nascent family champions can seek out education to help them manage their situations. Or they might be inspired through educational content to take on more influential roles in their families.

The opportunity to learn from other business families and professionals at conferences, seminars, or other events can be an influential experience for would-be or current family champions. As one family champion said, "I started going to family-business forums to hear experts on the field talk. It was like they were a fly on the wall in our family, and I thought, 'How do they know so much about us?'"

His words highlight the many elements common to family businesses, such that opportunities to meet other business families help champions realize (1) they are not alone in their quests and challenges, (2) there are many resources to help them succeed, and (3) other families have dealt successfully with ownership development. So it's no surprise that family champions often return from educational events brimming with ideas, information, and enthusiasm to share with family members.

What do family champions do?

Family champions act through a series of interrelated processes that have a positive impact on the entire family. We view this process as an ongoing *Cycle of Engagement*—a positive feedback loop that is dynamic, iterative (self-influencing), and ever-evolving.

Figure 7: Cycle of Engagement

Encompassing different types of activities, the cycle is aimed at helping owners work through dynamics and other issues to make progress on vision, governance, accountability, and other key areas.

The cycle helps both the individual and the family to evolve. Sometimes, in motivating the family to move toward champion status, the family champion can increase their commitment and help them find resources to develop enhanced ownership perspective and skills. As the family evolves into a champion family, this effort also enables individual family champions to take their skills and impact to the next level, in an ongoing and mutually beneficial cycle.

Families do not necessarily go through the cycle in exactly the same sequence depicted here. The components and order can differ widely, depending on particular elements of the family situation, and many activities can be carried out in parallel. The general concept of cyclical activity is similar across families. The most effective family champions and champion families continuously learn from their work and adjust the cycle of influence naturally and readily to meet their needs.

Cycle of Engagement components

Here are some definitions and explanations of these components:

Providing leadership. The point where the family champion begins to exert influence on the system, usually the result of one of the shift points described earlier. The champion injects energy into the ownership group, typically through family council or informal family meetings. The family champion becomes the inspiration and engine of change, helping the family develop in positive ways on multiple fronts: communication, relationships, decision-making, and others. This is the starting place for action.

Enhancing communication. To start the development efforts, family champions commonly improve communication patterns with family members, as was the case especially with Sofia and Lawrence from our examples. In fact, in many cases the dysfunctional communication patterns contribute directly to the need for a family champion, and the patterns exist in the first place because the absence of family leadership degrades communication.

Communication is fundamental to human relationships, and it forms the foundation of how we interact. Without effective communication, none of the family's other efforts can fully succeed.

Navigating family dynamics. In addition to improving communication, the family champion commonly works to manage the intergenerational and overall family dynamics. That means helping the generations work to understand one another both in language and perspective, and to integrate their experiences in a complementary manner. The family might work on improving other behavioral patterns where needed, as Carla did with her tactless relative, or as the Thompson cousins did with the substance-abusing family employee.

Unhealthy family dynamics can be critical and challenging. To address them, the family champion must confront the issues directly and model healthy behavior. An outside professional might be valuable, because the family champion is limited by working within the family system. People who specialize in family dynamics, communication, and family systems theory can help the family specifically address their challenges and build healthy family interactions.

Empowering others. Family champions cannot do this work alone, so they work to empower others. They actively engage them and bring them deeper into the process of increasing family communication and connecting members to their shared legacy. The family champions also encourage the entire family to build alignment through their actions. Spreading the engagement throughout the system is a key part of building positive momentum and effectiveness for the family.

Sofia did an excellent job of empowering others by drawing family members into various subcommittees and task forces. In one case, a family member raised the question, "Why don't we get a bigger dividend?" In response, Sofia asked that member to study the financial metrics of their company, compared to firms of a similar size. Other interested people formed a group that promised to report to the shareholder assembly in a year with their findings and recommendations. The group was both chagrined and pleased to report that, in fact, their family was receiving a generous dividend, given the business's finances. Hearing this from the task force was much easier for the ownership group than hearing the same thing from the patriarch. In general, having an engaged and empowered shareholder group investigate specific issues and make recommendations can be a powerful way to make progress as an ownership group.

Resolving challenges. For family champions, challenges are inevitable. But their work helps to shift the outlook and culture of the family to view challenges as opportunities, and not to let them derail the overall process. All of the champions presented earlier helped their families develop more adaptive, forward-looking cultures and outlooks.

Creating shared vision. Many family champions realize that the family has no unified vision about ownership. So the champion asks key questions: "Where are we going?" "What are our goals?" "Where do we want to be in 20 years?" "What is our vision as a group, including the views and interests of all generations, not just senior ones?" Questions like these help the family co-create an aligned vision of where they are going and why they are doing the work to get there. The family can't achieve any meaningful goals without a guiding sense of vision. So the family champion is pivotal in helping to formulate and refine a collective vision, as Carla did to arrive at her family's True North story.

Integrating education. The family champion can also serve as an educational resource for the family in multiple ways:
- Bring in pertinent informational resources such as books or articles
- Recruit professionals to focus on specific topics such as governance or leadership
- Bring groups to family business conferences, where they can learn from experts and other families

Mechanisms of engagement

Families are complex systems, and moving them in a positive direction requires effort and interactive processes on many fronts. We see that family champions are most effective when they are consistent, clear, and broad in their efforts. Here are a number of complementary approaches that support the components in the cycle of engagement:

Informal mechanisms are the daily interactions that take place between family champions and their family. Although casual, they are far from unimportant. In fact, sometimes it's the emails, phone calls, and contacts that take place between the formal meetings that matter most. Sofia, for example, refused to engage in the dysfunctional email exchanges common in her family. Instead, she picked up the phone and talked to people directly about sensitive topics related to ownership and family dynamics. No one told her to do this. It was something she had to do to stop old patterns and integrate new, healthier ways of interacting. Similarly, Lawrence took an initially informal approach to understanding his family's ownership-related opinions and perspective. He reached out to a few members in each generation with preliminary questions and, encouraged by their interest and openness, proposed a more formal effort to talk to all members.

Formal mechanisms are roles that champions take on after growing beyond an informal position. Champions often start with informal roles and begin interacting with the broader family because the system needs it. As they demonstrate their value and importance, they often take on more formalized responsibilities. Given the nature of business families, the most common starting place for a family champion is a spot on the family council. In fact, many family champions earn their way into serving as the family council chair. In families without a family council, some of the family champion's early efforts might go toward creating this governance structure. The champion might logically assume the role as chair, to sustain the effort. From these formalized positions, family champions are able to use their influence in a more codified, systematic, positive manner. The formality of the role lends some degree of authority, but family chair is still not typically a hierarchical position. Family champions must always be aware that their work is one of influence, not command. Carla represents a great example of influence over authority, because her position as youngest third-generation member gave her little hierarchy-based power.

A key element of leading a family ownership group, distinct from leadership of the business: The family champion's role as a leader is largely a position of positive influence.

Catalyst action is driving important change and helping to keep things running. Through both formal and informal mechanisms, family champions are catalysts. They use their motivation and inspiration to bloom the system more fully, providing critical energy and direction for success. Their work throughout the cycle of engagement constantly catalyzes the work of the family in a way that makes the best use of everyone's energy and engagement. They also help to establish or reaffirm the structures and culture to drive positive change and manage conflict effectively rather than avoiding it. To do this work alone would result in burnout, so a true family champion acts in multiple ways to harness the capabilities of the entire family to make contributions.

In all of these ways, family champions engage the family in a positive, continuous cycle. They foster ownership development and all the benefits that a more active, informed group of owners can drive. This positive influence has a direct correlation to the success of the business itself. This is how, as we show in later chapters; family champions create champion families.

Questions to consider

- We have presented multiple characteristics of typical family champions, including commitment to the family, interpersonal skills, and ability to build credibility and trust. Which of your family members do you see with strong potential in these areas?
- Are any family members (including you) acting as family champions currently? What are they (or you) doing?
- Which extended-family members have experience—professional, nonprofit, or others—that might help them enhance the ownership group in meaningful ways? How?
- What potential shift-points, such as a leadership transition or void, is your family facing that might intensify the need for a family champion? Who among your family members can serve as a resource to help manage this transition?
- What educational resources might the family draw on to develop owners further, including books, formal programs, or mentorship from other families?
- Take a look at the Cycle of Engagement we presented earlier. What stage or stages does the family seem to be in? What aspects can you work on further, now or in the near future?
- In what informal ways might your family owners develop further, especially in terms of improved communication or information-sharing among members?

CHAPTER 3: CHAMPION FAMILIES

Inspirational family businesses create success across generations

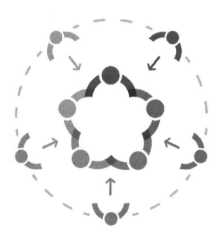

To illustrate the concept of champion families, we're going to introduce you to a few of them. These examples demonstrate commonalities and defining features that we explore in later discussions.

CHAPTER 3

The proactive Andersons

On the outskirts of a small Midwestern town is a billion-dollar business with diversified holdings in professional services, construction, and real estate. The Anderson family owns an enterprise that includes more than 15 companies with operations in three states. The business family now includes three generations. Five siblings of the second generation—two sisters and three brothers, all in their late 40s to late 50s—lead the business with the assistance of a team of talented non-family executives. The founding generation is no longer active in day-to-day operations, but the patriarch is active in identifying new business opportunities. Three third-generation members and two in-laws work in the business as well. The Andersons are philanthropic, and family members sit on multiple nonprofit boards.

For years, various family members have empowered others to become more effective owners or to establish the next level of family or business governance. The family recently formed a continuity planning committee including the matriarch, patriarch, all five second-generation siblings, Chief Financial Officer, estate planning attorney, and their family business advisor to develop a multiyear plan for ownership and leadership succession. The Andersons created the committee when the older second-generation siblings realized they needed to plan for their own leadership succession and move out of an operating role within five to seven years. Additionally, the size of the fast-rising third generation (15 members, the oldest in their mid-20s) means it's critical to educate and integrate these new owners into the governance process.

Along with this effort, the Andersons are moving to streamline operating agreements, update trusts and estate plans, and ensure representation of all branches and generations on the family council. "We made a list of things we wanted to work on and it just kept growing," one family leader said.

Following the lead of their parents and grandparents, two cousins in the third generation stepped up and organized monthly meetings where the cousins discuss business and family matters. Their goal is to become more informed, capable stewards. Each meeting has a structured agenda with agreed-upon discussion topics. Building on the education programs they attend at their family's annual stakeholder retreat, several of the older cousins volunteered to study one of their operating companies and prepare a high-level update. In addition to helping them understand the family's business, this exercise allows them to demonstrate and build their skills.

On the business governance side, the Andersons are developing a formal holding-company advisory board that includes the founders, all second-generation siblings, and outside advisors. This group will evolve into a fiduciary board with independent directors. In thinking about any of these efforts, the family considers implications within and across the three circles of family enterprise—family, business, ownership (see Chapter 1) and adjusts their strategies accordingly.

All siblings live within easy driving distance of one another, and the extended family meets often for holidays, barbecues, and other family events. These get-togethers feature a balance of casual conversation and shop talk. Rory, the younger second-generation sister, has emerged as a family leader, the one the others trust to *go talk to Dad* about difficult questions or issues. As chair of the family council, she has become adept at managing business and family challenges within and across generations. "I tell people my door is always open to talk about anything," Rory says.

Beyond such casual interactions, the family also has a conflict resolution policy that stipulates members do their best to work out issues among themselves first, and then to escalate as needed to an impartial person within or outside the family. So far, the system has worked well to foster healthy resolution and avoid the buildup of resentment. The Andersons continue reaping the material and intangible rewards of their enterprise.

The evolving Grubers

We highlight the Grubers, not because they have completed their evolution, but because they are in the process of becoming responsible, influential owners. They are a champion family because they actively engage across the seven key areas for success: leadership, purpose, values, governance, education, communication, and relationships.

Based in the western US, Gruber Enterprises started in the 1940s as a construction and infrastructure business that diversified quickly to take advantage of the West's growing population and economy. They moved from the construction core into ventures including real estate development, investment partnerships, and agriculture. A third-generation family member is the current CEO, and both the business and family are enjoying strong growth and its benefits.

The family ownership group has evolved along with the business. The owners are largely in the third generation, but the fourth generation is emerging into young adulthood and beginning to learn about trusts, trustee-beneficiary relationships, and ownership responsibilities.

Years ago, the third-generation cousins created an eight-person family council. All council members pursue separate careers, including medicine, academia, and entrepreneurship. The result is a diverse and capable council with a high level of discussion and contribution. The cousins on the council represent all three primary family branches, but have worked hard to move away from a branch mentality. They look out for the good of the *entire* system with a long-term view, and their work is gaining momentum.

Through their work on the council, the cousins pursue family development initiatives centered on education, governance, philanthropy, entrepreneurship, and social-relational opportunities. They pass on ownership knowledge and capabilities to the fourth generation, their children. At the same time, the family is working to broaden their business governance. The component companies have been run successfully with small, family-based boards, but the current CEO would like to systematically expand them to include independent members.

The Grubers have accomplished a great deal. Although they have a long way to go, it is their dedication and investment that makes them a champion family.

The Andersons and the Grubers are not perfect—no family is. But they exemplify the champion family, one that manages much of the complexity of family enterprise and achieves some real successes. They realize that the journey has no defined end point, and they continue to work on issues within the three circles of family business and their intersections.

This chapter shifts the focus from family champions, or the individuals who drive progress on enterprise issues for the family (see Chapter 2), to the *champion families* that often emerge from their efforts. Based on key insights we've gained from our experiences, let's look at what it takes to get there.

What makes a champion family?

As our examples suggest, a champion family is typically a larger multigenerational family that successfully manages complexity and performs well as a large, growing ownership group. These families have learned to deal with the difficult challenges of family enterprise in a variety of areas. They do not rest on their laurels or revenues. Instead, they proactively invest in ongoing development at all levels, with special attention to leadership, planning, and governance.

The proactive Andersons are a good example of a champion family because they are constantly in motion—building on existing structures, knowledge, and processes to prepare for an even brighter future. In the language of management expert Peter Senge, they are a *learning organization*: one that strives for continuous self-improvement through self-reflection and intention, nurturing new patterns of thinking, supporting collective aspiration, and maintaining a results orientation.[6]

Champion families can be defined in broad terms, but they also share notable hallmarks. These hallmarks, introduced in Chapter 1, make up the *foundational* elements of success for business families. This assessment is based on our extensive personal experience working with families, as well as established perspectives from colleagues through the field of family enterprise consulting.[7] Each element helps promote performance, continuity, and family harmony. As with everything we present in this book, consider this list as it pertains to you and your family. In which areas are you already well developed? Where do you see opportunity to grow?

Sofia's champion family

The individual efforts of Sofia, one of the family champions profiled in Chapters 1 and 2, have helped her family become a well-developed, continuously evolving champion family. The family, based in the southeastern US, has owned a growing manufacturing business for nearly a century.

Sofia's family demonstrates the seven characteristics of champion families, in *italics* in the passage below, introduced in Chapter 1 and shown in Figure 8.

Currently, the family has clear *leadership* for both the family (Sofia) and the business (a non-family CEO and chairman of the board). In addition, the collective family has worked hard to develop and agree on an inspiring *purpose* for their actions: to honor and perpetuate the family legacy and

---

[6] For more on learning organizations see Senge, P. (2005). *The fifth discipline: The art and practice of the learning organization.* New York, NY: Doubleday.

[7] As detailed in Chapter 1, we have drawn and built on the work of family business experts including Randel Carlock, John L. Ward, Danny Miller, Isabelle Le Breton-Miller, and Dennis Jaffe in defining the characteristics of champion families.

build opportunities for the future. This purpose is supported by a clearly defined set of *values* that guide the family's decisions and actions—for both the family and business—that include integrity, trust, and transparency. Informed by these values, the family created efficient and functional *governance* structures with a well-developed board of directors, including independent members and competent, qualified family members. They also have a seven-member representative family council that helps to organize the 50 family-owners.

One champion family might differ markedly from another on the traits profiled here (as our example families illustrate). But, while maintaining distinct profiles, these families typically share the view that their work is ongoing, and that the work builds on itself in a beneficial cycle.

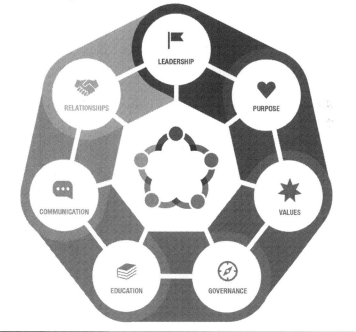

Figure 8: Seven key hallmark elements of champion families

To foster members' growth as capable owners and stewards, the family invests in initiatives for their own *education* by contributing 1% of their dividend. *Communication* was a challenge for the family when Sofia rose as a champion, and it became one of her top priorities. With Sofia's help, the family developed good standards of communication, moving from passive-aggressive interactions to more honest, open, and productive ones. "We talk much more constructively now," one of the third-generation cousins said. "Even about hard things."

Better communication helped the family repair *relationships* that had been strained in the second generation. The third-generation cousins knew they did not want to perpetuate the harmful family dynamics of their parents, so they worked hard to form new bonds and ways of interacting on their own terms.

These changes have been challenging, of course, requiring a significant investment of time and energy. With Sofia's help, the family learned how to compromise more effectively and to build consensus. Sofia's individual leadership was bolstered by the improved family interactions. Individuals were encouraged to take on greater engagement and development, and the large group benefited in the short term. For example, they provided greater educational opportunities and a clearer path to governance for interested family members.

One of the most critical steps was development of a strong, effective family owners council. Sofia worked to help raise the expectations, qualifications, and overall function of the family council. Although it's called a family council, theirs is truly an ownership council, because it functions as an influential liaison between the family owners and the business itself.

Sofia also helped develop the board of directors, working with several task forces of family members to create a list of competencies and qualifications for family board membership. She delegated responsibilities and tasks to the groups based on who was capable and interested, thus spreading the workload and accountability. The task forces produced clear guidelines for how to develop family members for specific governance roles and how to identify non-family candidates for independent director roles. Sofia also served as a pivotal member of the director committee that searched and placed several qualified independent board members. She helped attract and retain talented, experienced leaders who share their business expertise to help the business succeed.

In a recent phone call, Sofia updated us on the family's progress. "We're far from done," she said, stressing how much ongoing commitment and effort is required to maintain and build on the gains the family has made. For example, the family recently banded together to protect the business from devastating estate tax implications when transferring ownership between generations. To ensure the longevity of the business, the family moved business ownership from individual trusts into a perpetual trust. They likely avoided having to sell the business to cover the tax liability. Family members made personal sacrifice as they faced the challenge, worked hard, and made decisions based on complex information.

"There's no way we could have made this kind of progress if we hadn't done all the hard work that came before," Sofia said. She added, "Things are not perfect, and we have the same personality challenges we always have, but we are so much better at managing ourselves and getting to the best decisions for us all."

Sofia also noted the challenge of keeping family members engaged and committed to their work. She said they have a large pool of interested family members, but a smaller number are truly committed to doing the work it takes to be qualified, contributing family members in their governance structures. She also shared that the family has encountered a new challenge with a shared vacation home left in trust by her grandparents. She expressed some frustration that they had come so far in certain areas, only to face disagreement over something that seemed so simple. Still, she remains optimistic: "We have overcome so many challenges that I trust us to get through this latest one. But I continue to find remarkable just how much effort it takes to make everything work."

Sofia's efforts as a family champion have been crucial in helping her family develop the key capabilities needed to be a champion family. But they have not crossed some imaginary finish line, nor do they believe they have—or ever will. The family members continue to sharpen their ability to work together and manage new challenges. Even as they develop greater competence, they need to continue to reinvest on multiple levels as they grow and evolve.

The seven elements and your family

Each element was highlighted with *italics* in Sofia's case. These order of these elements, shown in Figure 8, is not significant. Some are easier to manage or improve upon than others, depending on your family's membership and situation. Think about how these elements appear in your family and where you recognize weaknesses.

Champion families tend to exhibit strength in these areas:

Leadership— have distinct leaders for the business and family. This leadership group works together in a complementary fashion, while also respecting boundaries between family and business. Separate but complementary leadership specific to each area ensures greater effectiveness and efficiency. Rory Anderson led the family council, her older brother was the business CEO, and they spoke frequently in both formal and informal settings to identify and resolve issues together. Sofia led her family, and a non-family CEO led the business.

Good leadership helps champion families excel at the business of the family. Chapter 2 covered the ways family champions help to run the family, whether organizing regular meetings or smoothing over disputes. Leading a family, unlike leading the business, involves working in a non-hierarchical system, with a more democratic, consensus-based approach.

Purpose—align with and rally around a clear, compelling sense of purpose. This sense of purpose gives meaning to the work the family invests in. *Vision* is closely related to purpose, and we believe that having a clear vision is essential to champion families because it gives direction and inspires action. There is an old saying, "When you don't know where you're going, any road will take you there."

Purpose provides that direction and helps to support the development of what we call *patient capital*. This term refers to how business families approach their finances with long-term thinking and perspective. It allows them to make decisions with a far-horizon time frame. An aligning vision is a key factor in producing successful results.

Values—have clearly defined values that serve as guiding principles. Much has been written about the importance of values in family businesses.[8] Purpose gives direction, but values help provide the *why* for doing the work and guide decisions about family employment, ownership, and conflict resolution. Values evolve from family culture, and they inform and perpetuate it. Values shape how family members treat one another and other stakeholders (employees, customers, suppliers, and the broader community). Sofia's family made the values of integrity, trust, and transparency explicit.

Governance— build strong governance structures. Governance is a broad term for an organized way to guide a group of people and to make decisions together. Governance applies to the family (a family council or ownership council) and business (board of directors). These structures work together but have distinct areas of focus. Family members can serve on both, connecting family and business productively.

---

[8] For more on the nature and role of values in family enterprise, see Aronoff, C.E., & Ward, J.L. (2011). *Family business values: How to assure a legacy of continuity and success.* New York, NY: Palgrave Macmillan US.

The Andersons had a working family council in place and are taking steps to enhance it—ensuring and boosting representation among branches and generations—while creating an advisory board (and eventual fiduciary board) for the holding company. This level of organization helps the family make decisions effectively together.

Another family we know, the Reeds, emphasized a democratic process in deciding—as the founder neared retirement—whether to sell a portion of their aerospace business. They met regularly and shared leadership of the process to reach a strong consensus about selling part of the business, thus running the family in a way that benefited both family and business. Governance in champion families is built

---

Fair process in champion families

- *No surprises.* Everyone know the issues and the call for decisions beforehand.
- *No conflicts of interest.* Personal interest and agendas are disclosed.
- *No side meetings or conversations.* Decisions are made transparently.
- *No rush.* All feel they have time to prepare and time to present their views.
- *Respect.* Each participant has equal opportunity to share and be heard.
- *Mutual commitment.* Genuine effort is made to find win-win solutions.
- *Good conduct.* If family meetings were videotaped and shown to future generations, the process depicted would make everyone proud.
- *Post-decision review.* Everyone has a chance to share a personal view of the process and review the results of the decision.

Figure 9: Fair process in champion families[9]

on a principle of fair process.

Education—strive for growth on many levels, build a culture around learning. Champion families recognize the complexity and challenge of caring for a family enterprise. Through continuing education for both family and individuals, they create a culture of growth and development. The family might bring in educators, consultants, and professionals to introduce specific content. They foster educational opportunities for family members of all ages and generations. Some families support international travel, personal development courses, and artistic pursuits as ways of expanding the experiences of individuals, and thus, the entire family.

The influx of education makes the entire family stronger and better able to meet their responsibilities as a business family. Education is approached with a long-term view. Investment in individual and collective development occurs over years, with focus on leadership, ownership, and wellness.

Communication—interact effectively. Champion families pay close attention to how they communicate and interact. For some families, working on communication is the single most important activity, one that's foundational in nature. Effective communication and fair process (see Figure 9) produce a culture of meaningful interaction, trust, transparency, and open-mindedness. Champion families often have communication agreements that address codes of conduct and provide policies, guidelines, explicit standards, and expectations.

Relationships—recognize the importance of strong interpersonal relationships and promote them. Families who love and feel affection for one another are more willing

---

[9] For more on fair process in family business, see Carlock, R.S., &. Ward, J.L. (2010). *When family businesses are best: The parallel planning process for family harmony and business success.* New York, NY: Palgrave Macmillan US.

to do the hard work of being owners together. In looking at the failures of business families, poor relationships and family dynamics are common contributors to strife, failure, and negative outcomes. Respect and strong relationships produce and sustain the bonds that make family members *want* to be together for a greater good. "I deeply love my family and want us to be wildly successful together," one business family member we know said. "Not just in the business, but in the family."

Of course, love alone is not enough to make a champion family. But we believe it's a sustaining component of long-lasting families. Often, family members think of how their decisions will affect their children and grandchildren. Love powers and shapes these decisions.

An investment in good relationships helps champion families manage their discord productively. Families inevitably have disagreements—it goes with the territory. But champion families resolve conflict in a fair and inclusive way. They strive for greater trust and better relationships through healthy resolution. The Andersons' conflict-resolution policy helped them embody this champion-family characteristic. They know that the element of *family-ness* is essential to running the family successfully.

Champion families also pay close attention to how their interactions across business, social, and financial domains affect their collective well-being. They make adjustments for the good of the group where needed, working effectively across the three circles of family enterprise. The Andersons' geographic proximity helped them gather frequently for formal and informal events, and they genuinely enjoyed their time together.

Multigenerational families might have three (or even four) generations working together. They grew up in different eras and probably have different worldviews and cultural instincts. Champion families make the most of these differences and encourage cross-generational sharing of perspectives and insights. The leaders glean wisdom and experience from older family members, and they also incorporate the views of their younger (digital native) members who are growing up in a rapidly changing world. Similarly, they strive to manage other forms of diversity, such as those related to wealth, ownership, and geographic dispersion. They see these as collective sources of strength rather than individual differences, boosting their sense of *we*.

A continuum, rather than stages

Although champion families reflect strengths on these qualities, don't assume they all look the same. For each key element, every family falls somewhere on a continuum from *good enough* to *great*, resulting in a unique profile. This contrasts with a *stage-type* model, where we could place each family in a specific category overall or for each element.

Two champion families, for example, might have different strengths in these key areas. But they both share a sense of commitment to be responsible owners, improve their collective capabilities, and make a positive impact as the ownership group. Thus each element represents a moving target, with the family growing by degrees through their efforts. There can be system-level strength even if all seven areas aren't fully developed, and families can be considered champion-level under a variety of circumstances. But if a business is truly thriving, all seven characteristics are integrated in some fashion.

The idea of *punctuated equilibrium*[10] applies here too. The family might look the same on one element such as leadership or governance for a long time, then improve significantly in a relatively short time due to greater commitment, involvement of members, and development of new skills through education and other means.

Along with strengths on the seven elements and commitment to developing their capabilities, the champion families we've observed exhibit these behaviors:

---

[10] An evolution theory that new species evolve suddenly over short spans of time, with long periods when little change occurs.

They seek the advice and guidance of trusted advisors. Champion families don't try to handle all challenges alone. They understand the value that outside advisors can bring on financial, succession, governance, and other issues. The most effective families collaborate with advisors to create policies, practices, and communication, in service of family harmony and business longevity.

They share their experience with other families. Champion families exchange success and challenge stories with other business families. They know their work can serve as both education and inspiration to other families, and they are alert to lessons that can be learned—even from another's struggles. They willingly share in forums such as peer groups, conferences, magazine articles, and informal conversations.

They take a proactive approach. The proactive Andersons in our example exemplify a willingness to invest in their development *ahead of the curve*, rather than in reaction to changes or stresses. Part of a proactive approach is taking advantage of resources in the family business field, whether through structured learning experiences or the engagement of outside advisors representing multiple skill sets. These families muster all resources available to survive and learn from challenging transitions, setbacks, and even successes.

They foster personal development. Champion families encourage members to pursue personal development based on their individual interests and needs. They recognize that family members can contribute best when they enjoy life on their own terms and based on their own passions, rather than pursuits or responsibilities imposed by the broader family. Personal development is a broad term that encompasses life experience, formal and informal education, and the cultural value of pursuing individual growth. It can include anything from creative writing courses to volunteer work to the performing arts to a spiritual calling.

Beware the black hole of the founder

James Hughes, Susan E. Massenzio, and Keith Whitaker write of the "Black Hole of the Founder," or the idea that business families orient so strongly around the dream and vision of the founders that they fail to develop their own aspirations and dreams. This needn't be something imposed upon rising generations or even a conscious process. Sometimes it happens because the founder is a strong personality or visionary. Families can guard against this by including measures to bring out individual interests, visions and ideas as part of a comprehensive Family Championship Plan (FCP).

Figure 10: Black hole of the founder

To promote personal development, some families have specific funding and other means to enable members to take advantage of travel, special opportunities, and other ways of enriching themselves. In turn, this helps members become strong, independent people who can make the *choice* to be involved with the business, rather than seeing it as a default option or obligation.

They encourage personal interests and entrepreneurship. The strongest champion families have found a way to foster personal interests and an entrepreneurial spirit among individual members as a way to sustain the family legacy. They recognize that not everyone in the family shares the dream of the founder[11]. By promoting the entrepreneurial ideas and goals of the rising generation, they expand and build the strength of the family through diversification.

---

[11] Hughes, J., Massenzio, S.E., & Whitaker, K. (2014). Voice of the rising generation. Hoboken, NJ: Wiley.

They have their finances in order. Large business families tend to amass significant financial assets, with growing complexity. Good estate planning, tax management, financial acumen, and wealth education are all important for their ongoing success and harmony. In the Reed family example, careful management of their finances and assets eased the decision to sell a portion of the business and facilitated its implementation in view of an upcoming succession.

How governance evolves in a champion family

Champion families are distinct from one another in key areas, but they tend to share similar paths of evolution, especially as they relate to family, ownership, and business governance. So it's worth taking a look at this specific similarity.

In general, champion families move to increasingly elaborate structures and processes that help them manage their complexity in a defined and effective manner. In this section we discuss some of the key governance steps in ascending order of organization and sophistication, but families differ in the path that's best for them.

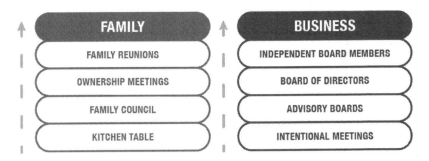

Figure 11: The evolution of governance

Most champion families go through these steps in the three overlapping circles (family, ownership, business) of the general family enterprise model. Keep in mind that this is a stylized view of champion families, and that not every family passes through these phases in the same sequence or with the same priorities.

Most families don't start with a formal *family council*. For many, the family council begins as a kitchen-table meeting, and evolves over time in organization and function. It gradually becomes an official family council that addresses many issues at the family-business intersection and ensures representation for branches and generations. At this point, many families begin with a single, all-purpose council that attends to both ownership and familial matters, and then develop it over time along separate paths that lead to distinct ownership and family councils. These specialized councils allow more specific focus and purpose.

Whether or not the family has a formal ownership council, *shareholder or ownership meetings* focus on matters of ownership, including discussion of financial returns, presentation of business performance information, and conversations about tax consequences. These meetings typically include only a subset of the extended family, because not all family members are owners.

The family council might oversee *family education initiatives* that develop individual and collective capabilities and perspective related to ownership, business, governance, and leadership. For example, they bring in educators, send family members to conferences, or develop an educational curriculum and delivery system.

More general *family meetings or reunions* are not limited to owners, and can have a purely social purpose such as ensuring branches and cousins get to know one another. These meetings can also be social and ownership-related, although formal shareholder meetings would fall under the ownership area. As families get larger and more geographically dispersed, a family retreat can serve as the primary point of contact for the extended family.

Alongside the evolution of family and ownership governance, business governance evolution tends to follow a typical path. Structures and processes move from an *advisory board* (potentially starting as informal and becoming more formal, with paid members), to a *fiduciary board of directors*, to the *addition of independent board members*, sometimes even a majority-independent board. Similarly, the proportion of family directors on the board tends to decline as the governance body evolves.

Sofia's family, the Andersons, and the Grubers are all good examples of evolution on the governance trait of family championship.

Key insights about champion families

Now that we have a clearer understanding of champion families and their seven core characteristics, we can share more specific insights about how they operate. Note the importance of the interaction and productive dynamics with champion families' individual counterparts: the family champions.

The concepts of champion families and family champions are both related and independent. A champion family might well be the result of the work of a family champion. We see this often, when an individual has invested significant energy in building the family-owners group. This was the case with several of the family champions we profiled in Chapter 2, including Sofia the Strategist and Carla the Coach. Each took the lead in developing her family's capacities, and fellow members gained enthusiasm and ability for pushing the group's skills further. Champion families do not develop overnight or by accident. They emerge as the result of hard work of many different people, and usually over several years.

There is an ongoing dance between individual and group dynamics. A champion family exemplifies the positive influence of the group on the individual and vice versa. In many cases, an individual—often a family champion—brings the system along under big picture questions such as: What do we really want as a family? What is our vision, and how do we achieve it? What are our greatest strengths and our most important challenges? As more members contribute to the effort to answer these questions, the movement of energy between individual and group becomes self-perpetuating and mutually beneficial. The example of Sofia's family illustrates this individual-group dynamic.

Governance is the conduit for information throughout the system. Governance represents the structure, process, and formal means for the exertion of influence by both family champions and champion families. For example, family champions often play key roles as the interface between the family or ownership council and the board of directors. They convey the values, culture, and intent of the family to the business. Champion families are largely made through these governance structures, and family champions are able to exert their continuing positive influence through them. The interplay of individual and group continues through the governance structures, for the benefit of the entire system.

Governance is not only a channel for influence but also a means to provide fair process for important decision-making, a critical ingredient in champion families. You might not always get your way, but if you have an opportunity to influence a decision and you believe the decision process was fair, you are more likely to go along with the decision. Champion families recognize this and seek to build fair process into their governance and other systems.

Champion families are interdependent systems. People and processes, formal and informal, form a system between them. Champion families appreciate the system, including the constant, often subtle movement of energy, interdependence, and mutual influence. As with any system, it's important for those within it to understand, not just the individual components, but also the interaction and interdependence of all the parts.

Champion families proactively adopt a systems-thinking approach in either style or formality because it helps them manage their complexity and dynamics. Family champions understand systems and sharpen their abilities to identify systems issues, exert more positive impact, and work to improve system functioning on multiple levels. We highlight the importance of a systems view because of the strong and pervasive interaction among so many complex aspects involved in business families. Knowledge of how systems work is an important attribute for family champions and anyone engaged in a champion family.

Questions to consider

- What does the concept of a champion family mean to you and how does it relate (or not relate) to your family?
- Where does your family, or one you advise, fall on the seven key characteristics of champion families? In which areas have you made the most progress? Which require the most attention?
- Champion families have built structures, processes, and capabilities related to business and family governance, leadership, financial management, conflict resolution, and other areas. On which of these has your family made the most progress? What areas deserve priority for development?
- Champion families evolve on key dimensions including the family, ownership, and business. Where is your family in this evolutionary scheme? What steps can be taken to promote further evolution in any of these three areas?
- What is the interplay of individual and group dynamics in your family, both positive and negative? How could the interplay be enhanced, based on concepts related to family champions and champion families?
- What are the systems elements in your own family that create opportunities? What systems elements create the largest challenges?

CHAPTER 4: DEVELOPING LEADERSHIP

Where do family champions come from?

The theme for this chapter could be "Family champions are made and born." We believe that becoming a family champion involves a combination of:

- Natural, innate talents, interests, and motivation
- Learnable skills that can be fostered by the right environment and encouragement
- The right opportunities, as promoted by preparation and, often, a dash of fortunate circumstance—or being in the right place at the right time

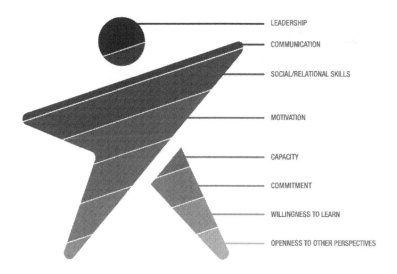

Figure 12: Family champion attributes

Being a family champion takes a lot of work, has uncertain return, and requires unique skill sets. It is not the sort of position you can prepare for in school. Still, some family champions emerge naturally in an evolving act of self-determination. Others can be developed from high-potential individuals given a push or motivation at the right time from someone in an advisory or mentorship role.

This chapter provides some tips for developing family champions so they can help develop and support the process of becoming a champion family. Even if you don't currently see potential champions in your family business environment or that of a family you advise, these concepts are important because they illustrate the emergence, growth, and hard work of family champions.

How to identify (potential) family champions

Even unlikely candidates can become family champions, including those not previously involved in ownership or governance issues. So how do you know if you or someone else in your family has the right stuff to be a family champion? To help you identify high-potential prospective champions, we offer a list of attributes (see Figure 12). Although Chapter 2 presented broad categories of family-champion qualities, we want to focus here on traits and behaviors that are easier to identify.

These qualities don't develop overnight. Family champions have usually been developing these capabilities from childhood, and they are likely bolstered during their careers and enhanced in their roles within the family enterprise. The attributes listed here are the most significant factors involved in family championship. We have observed them in a wide variety of family champions and families.

Leadership: Family champions show strong leadership capability, not limited to business or professional settings. It can include leadership in volunteer, sports, or religious activities, for example. We know family champions who first showed leadership as coaches, nonprofit board members, and missionaries. Lawrence, from the core example in this chapter, gained leadership skills running his restaurant-bar outside the family firm. Leaders tend to rise to their positions naturally. Because of their skills and influence, people look to them for direction.

Communication: Family champions communicate well. They listen and display a high degree of emotional intelligence.[12] They share their ideas in a way that enables other people to understand, feel inspired, and make their own contributions. Family champions are also adaptable, adjusting their communication styles to the audience. They face difficult conversations head-on, addressing sensitive topics in a respectful, effective manner. Sofia demonstrated emotional intelligence on multiple fronts. She enabled people to communicate more directly and respectfully, emphasized listening, and resolved long-standing disputes between family branches.

Social and relational skills: Family champions relate well to others. They have a genuine interest in getting to know people and understanding what motivates them. They are socially central: people gravitate toward them. They don't need to be extroverted or the life of the party, but they are thoughtful and generally charismatic. The emotionally intelligent person tends to command attention through character, building credibility, trust, and rapport, rather than through attention-seeking behavior. Lawrence's listening skills helped the extended-family members feel supported and respected. They were able to share their vision for the family's future and their roles in it.

---

[12] Goleman, D. (2005). *Emotional Intelligence*. New York, New York: Bantam Books.

What is emotional intelligence?

Emotional intelligence, also known as one's "emotional quotient" (EQ) is the ability to be aware of one's emotions and those of others, and to be able to harness this understanding, along with other interpersonal skills, to build relationships and motivate individuals and groups to take on challenges. While there are multiple ways to get at EQ, it is most easily observed informally, in how well a person gets along with others and makes them feel motivated and happy, rather than fearful or threatened.

A simple question that has been proposed to measure EQ is "Do your emotions ever work against you?" That is, do anger, frustration and anxiety tend to get the better of you in multiple situations? The more they do, the lower your EQ. Family champions tend to have naturally high EQ that increases with experience and attention. Their EQ is also reflected in their ability to empathize, or to take others' perspectives, especially in challenging situations such as conflicts. The ability to see situations from other points of view helps family champions to promote better understanding and accord among the broader family group.

Figure 13: Emotional intelligence

Motivation: Family champions don't just talk about doing something, they do it. Like Lawrence, their attitude is, "If I don't do it, nobody else will." But motivation is short-lived without perseverance. Family champions have drive and stamina, often accomplishing tasks despite inertia or resistance within the family system.

Capacity: Even with the other qualities here, family champions need time and mental capacity to take on the long-term challenge of developing an owner group. That's why family champions are often not the family business leaders. Business leaders focused on operating a healthy business rarely have the capacity to work on developing a healthy family as well. In Sofia's case, the demands of her role eventually expanded into a salaried position within the family. This channeled her full energy to the family and the CEO's to the business, with beneficial results for both.

Commitment: The family champion displays a commitment to the family's well-being over the long term. That means a given family champion's role might be temporary, but even if others pick up the torch and carry on during the family's evolution, commitment to the family's success is preserved. Sofia, Lawrence, and all other family champions demonstrate that the family champion acts on behalf of the whole, not an individual or sub-group.

Willingness to learn: Family champions realize that they have a lot to learn, and they seek development. This might mean education through books, conferences, leadership courses, or other resources (see a list in the Appendix). They are also willing learn from the family and, as Lawrence did, they solicit feedback. Family champions also pass on what they learn for the benefit of the family and the business.

Openness to other perspectives: Like the willingness to learn, an ability to be open to other perspectives is closely related to empathy (see Figure 13). Family champions know that a family's many different viewpoints are based on generation, ownership level, culture, geography, wealth, values, and other factors. The larger and more complex the family, the broader the range of opinions, the more important this openness becomes. As both Sofia and Lawrence note, this does not mean everyone always agrees. But a fair process helps create consensus.

As you think about who might make a good family champion in your family (maybe you?), read back through this list and consider whether the person in question matches well with these traits.

How the family champion supports the family business system

One of the most important aspects of family championship is the *interplay* between individuals and the broader family system. Family champions must navigate a system with multiple stakeholders (see Figure 1: The 3-Circle Model). That includes family, owners, managers, board members, employees, customers—the entire community of people affected by the work and actions of the family business. But the family champion works primarily in the interface between the family and business.

What works well in theory can be challenging in reality. The owning family is typically a group of people representing a diverse set of perspectives, preferences, and challenges. And the family champion must navigate these complexities to create an ownership group that directly benefits the business. The most successful family champions do not act as solo practitioners, but build collective effort by involving others. It is no surprise that successful family systems (those that achieve their goals most effectively) foster a healthy flow of energy between individual and group. Let's take another look at a family champion who illustrates this interaction.

Carla the Coach

We met Carla in Chapter 2. She's the youngest third-generation member of a Brazilian-American family that owns multiple businesses on the US west coast. While working outside the family firm as a financial professional, she became more involved in ownership issues and found, like Sofia and Lawrence, that she had an affinity for the work. For example, she led successful efforts to recruit independent board directors and worked to improve communication among generations and branches. "It was mostly about getting people in the same room so they could see their views weren't that different," she said.

Based on these efforts, Carla's family entrusted her with the role of family council chair. But her work was just beginning. Specifically, the family had no shared vision of what they wanted as owners, and thus no clearly articulated goals. What was the future they all aimed for? Did they want to steward the enterprise for the long-term? To generate individual liquidity by selling the businesses, in whole or part? Did they want to make the effort to be aligned as a group? It seemed as if they had lost their way. They wondered if alignment was even possible for them.

At first, Carla wrestled with these questions mostly on her own, but quickly realized she had to engage the larger family system. So she worked to provide inspiration to address these questions as a larger group, knowing that consensus would probably be difficult.

Carla took a two-pronged approach. First, recognizing there was only so much she could do within the family system on such large issues, she brought in an outside advisor. Right away, the advisor acted as a guide and facilitator, helping everyone understand the challenge of eliciting a unified, integrated vision from the broader family, and suggesting ways to make it happen. Together they discussed what processes to use and how, given the family's makeup and dynamics. The advisor also worked with Carla on her leadership, highlighting areas to strengthen—such as having difficult conversations when needed. They determined what efforts would benefit most from a more team-based leadership approach (such as developing task forces to explore specific vision elements). The advisor also helped her think through likely obstacles, including resistance and clashes among specific family members or branches.

Armed with this thinking, Carla organized a family retreat to grapple with the big question: What do we want as a family? Carla and the advisor served as co-facilitators, walking the family through multiple thought-provoking scenarios to reach a shared vision: Where are we going? What happens if we do nothing? What happens if we do *this*? What happens if we do *that*? Throughout, Carla urged her family to focus on a central, organizing question: "What is our most aspirational vision for ourselves?"

After long and sometimes difficult conversations, the family was able to agree on a compelling vision of stewardship. They called it their *True North Story*. The vision reduced ambiguity and uncertainty about the future, and it helped to motivate and energize the family to be more active owners. As a more aligned group, they even considered the roles and responsibilities they might take to achieve their goals.

Carla was proud of her family's ability to rise to the challenge of creating a vision. "I didn't agree with everything that came out of the retreat," she said. "But I was proud to see my family turn the potential I saw in them into a real plan, with a lot of commitment." As the family moves to realize the vision, Carla continues to shape their efforts as family council chair and, more recently, board director. These formal roles help her serve as a primary interface between the family and business systems, working hard to ensure mutual understanding and objectives.

"I know we have a strong vision," Carla says of the future. "The question now is how do we get there." Her family is fortunate to have a champion like her in the coaching role, helping them work as a team toward their goal, True North.

Figure 14: Developing the True North Story of a champion family

What makes it work

In most situations, several elements converge to help the individual and the family-business system work through a mutually beneficial interplay. Typically, it is set in motion by the champion and sometimes aided by outside advisors. Here are the primary ways family champions build and develop champion families:

Collective vision, transformational leadership: Family champions act on behalf of the whole system, not just themselves: They ask, "What is best for *us?*" That means the champion must take a holistic and *transformational leadership* approach, endeavoring to serve a larger cause.[13]

---

[13] For more on this important concept, see Vernon, A. (2015).

For example, Lawrence's listening tour helped him become a transformational leader because he made extended family members feel heard for the first time. He developed a clearer understanding and vision for what the family actually wanted. "After the tour we had a treasure-trove of information about what the shareholders were really interested in and thinking about," he said. The listening tour helped people feel valued, and the entire family system responded positively.

The best family champions are transformational leaders

Transformational leaders are those focused on transforming not only ambiguity into vision and vision into reality, but also transforming the team from a potentially passive or even resistant group into one committed to real, lasting change. Among the qualities that support transformational leadership are the ability to lead not just with the head but with the heart, to take an approach based on curiosity and playfulness even with regard to serious and high-stakes matters, and to use stories to inspire and inform others. Many family champions embody these as transformational leaders.

Figure 15: Transformational leaders

Developing the 3 habits of transformational leaders. *Forbes*, August 27, 2015. Retrieved from http://www.forbes.com/sites/yec/2015/08/27/developing-the-3-habits-of-transformational-leaders/#ca3aec11c45b

Empowerment of others: The family champion cannot do all of the work alone, and must continually act to empower other family members. Sometimes this means developing committed task forces of family members to take on specific challenges , as Sofia and Carla did. Sofia's commitment to a healthier family dynamic, for example, motivated several of her cousins to look past historical issues and join her in calling for better cross-branch relationships. "We saw her doing it and thought we should get involved too," a cousin said. That created positive shifts in patterns of family interactions— more communication and cooperation among cousins from different branches, for example—and that boosted Sofia's credibility. In general, such actions help to engage more family members, to gather their perspectives and energy, and to produce more sustainable results that motivate still others to get involved.

Engage outside support: Most family champions realize they can't do everything alone. They cannot always find the expertise or support they need within the broader family. So they are willing to recruit outside advisors—experts in law, business, accounting, governance, succession, or other fields. The advisor and champion make a stronger team, especially in stimulating difficult (but necessary) conversations. Carla's engagement of a capable outside advisor accelerated and enhanced her family's movement toward their shared True North vision.

Integration through appreciation: The champion acts to integrate preferences and points of view, as both Carla and Lawrence did in meaningful ways. Champions work to promote large variations in age, cultural background, ownership levels, as rich sources of diverse thinking—not as sources of conflict. They are able to elicit and assimilate opinions into a collective approach to challenges. The family champion then takes steps to integrate these multiple, diverse perspectives into a whole that respects the individuals and group. Through Lawrence's effort, for example, the family realized that most shareholders really enjoyed being part of the business. Once they saw the potential of working together on a variety of investment-related and other initiatives, they wanted to remain owners.

Formal and informal events: Family champions, sometimes with the help of outside advisors, use both formal and informal events to help families share views and reach shared vision and understanding. This might mean casual conversations (Sofia helped her family by getting them in the same room to resolve differences) or more formal events, such as Carola's retreat and Lawrence's listening tours.

Trust: In the end, success in business families often comes down to trust. Does the family trust the family champion to act in best interest? Does the family champion trust the family to pitch in with their efforts and ideas? Do the owners trust the managers of the business? All of the family champions and champion families we've observed have established deep trust in their relationships, allowing them to take on large, often contentious, challenges and to grow from both success and setback.

How the family system supports the champion

Champion families support the family champion as an integral aspect of their success. This support is *earned*, not just bestowed, and trust has to be earned with the entire array of individuals who make up the system. Families that support the role of the family champion through recognition and respect tend to succeed because they gain from the champion's full energy and efforts, boosting the family's abilities on multiple levels.

Figure 16: Supporting the champion

Next we consider both a positive and a negative example to show how the family can support (or fail to support) a potential champion.

Sofia's family support

Our earlier example of Sofia the Strategist illustrates the concept of family support. When Sofia began her work, she did so voluntarily. As her engagement grew, she became part of the family council, and eventually its chair. At the time of that transition, she was doing the work based on her desire to contribute to the family. She wanted to carry forth the family legacy and make sure the business continued to provide family members with increased equity and yearly dividends. As family council chair, Sofia knew that the family needed to do extensive work to develop itself. They were not ready to meet the ownership responsibilities of a rapidly increasing business under her father's successor, a non-family CEO with ambitious growth plans. When the family saw that the resources she needed to devote to this effort warranted full-time compensated work, Sofia's family offered her a salaried position focused on ownership issues. "It was clear she was adding a lot of value already," one family council member said. They approved paying her a salary similar to that of a mid-level manager in the organization.

The decision was both validation of the value she brought and an investment in the further development of the entire system, built on trust. Later, as she laid out her vision and plans, the family continued to provide backing in the form of active participation—even when that meant initial disagreement—and financial support. In this example we see how a champion family's active support of their family champion has significant, reciprocal positive effect.

For an opposite view, consider the example of aspiring family champion Gordon, whom the system did not ultimately support.

Gordon's struggle

Gordon, one of three second-generation siblings in a family-owned chemical engineering business, was a would-be family champion. He, his siblings, and their mother inherited a large portfolio of assets from their stepfather, the founder, including both liquid and illiquid (such as real estate) assets and intellectual property with long-term value. Gordon soon recognized that proper stewardship and potential monetization of the inherited assets would require the family to be better organized.

On paper, Gordon displayed the majority of the characteristics of a family champion as discussed in this book. He had a strong sense of purpose, and he was motivated to self-educate himself about what successful business families do. He also had strong communication and interpersonal skills. But as Gordon became more vocal and involved in efforts to organize the family, he faced several problems.

First, entrenched family dynamics became more problematic with the possibility of significant wealth. Gordon's brother and sister, a professor and a doctor, fought for territory with him. Each sought greater control over the assets. "Why should we trust you with this?" they said. They viewed themselves as more capable than their siblings. Making matters worse, Gordon's mother refused to move forward with any sort of organization or group decision-making process, in part because she believed she deserved a larger share of the inherited assets. She also stymied Gordon's efforts to seek professional guidance on their situation.

When his siblings and mother hired three separate attorneys to fight for control, Gordon lost his motivation to advance the family in their stewardship efforts. He ultimately became estranged from the family, taking his share of the inheritance and moving far from his home state, where he could insulate himself from the destructive family dynamics.

Gordon's unfortunate example shows that when family champions do not have the support of the system, their ideas, capabilities, and intentions don't matter. The family system must embrace and value the efforts of the would-be champion, or there will be no traction. In another example, the middle brother of the second generation tried to emerge as a family champion, but the system refused to empower him because his values around wealth were misaligned with the broader family's: he lived a more ostentatious, lavish lifestyle than they did, with multiple homes, cars, and boats. The family felt he didn't represent their core value of humility, and didn't trust him to act in their best interest. In this case, he *couldn't* have emerged as true family champion, because he was simply too different from his family on critical cultural and values.

CHAPTER 4

What makes it work

Here are several ways successful champion families support the family champion:

Structures of support: The family council often serves as the primary forum to help organize the family and provide a means to make decisions. The family council might have various sub-committees, such as education, events, finance, development, and others, that help broaden engagement and spread the workload. Assign task forces to help involve family members in specific projects. Construct the systems to have a good interaction among leadership, family council members, and owners.

Development focus: Healthy family business systems need to have the perspective and means to develop family members to be the best *people* and contributors they can be, regardless of their roles. The entire family and the business benefit when individuals invest in their own growth and development in accordance with their passions and goals. They are able to share experience, energy, and ideas into the family-ownership group, as Sofia did after attending the NextGen leadership program at Loyola University.

People move in and out of the family-ownership circles in different ways. Some are actively engaged, some pursue their careers as the main focus, and some drift in and out of engagement. In most healthy families, authenticity at the individual and group levels is highly valued.

Family members should pursue their *genuine* interests, with some consideration for how doing so could serve the family. For example, a creative writer can write novels, but can also consider writing the family newsletter. An attorney can pursue a law practice, but also lend the family legal insight and perspective. Families with good liquidity might also establish financial support for members on their development paths, with family-business-specific education, conferences, workshops, and networking.

Education: For the long-term success of family and business enterprises, developing a culture and ethos of ongoing education is important. Opportunities for knowledge-building, whether through formal programs at universities or informal interaction with other families, are abundant. Conferences, workshops, professional advisors, books, articles, and networking all provide ways to learn more about family-business systems.

Financial support: Many of the efforts we mention are supported by financial investment. Some families have a specific education fund, and others are less formal. Families who invest in their education and development as a culture tend to enhance family harmony and support ongoing business success. They continually bring in new information and ideas to improve their system-wide interactions. In other cases, financial support might mean paying a family champion as part of a formal role, as was the case for Sofia.

Culture: Families who are self-aware about celebrating their culture and values succeed at this vitally important aspect of being a business family. Cultures that support and encourage interactions across generations, branches, and all three circles of the family business model are more likely to result in success and harmony than those that don't. Culture includes the values, interactions, respect, and other elements of *how we do things as a family*. Cultures that value the role of the family champion and understand how this role interacts with the broader family system are more likely to support a champion's efforts and gain value from these people.

    Culture is the essential foundation for how the family operates together. Values determine what the family wants to achieve together, and the family champion provides the energy and focus to help the family formulate their goals and paths toward achieving them.

Points to keep in mind

The family champion concept has significant nuance, working with both family and business systems in a mutually supportive atmosphere. And the *champion family* results from an effective balance of these elements:

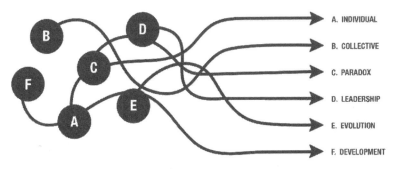

A. INDIVIDUAL

B. COLLECTIVE

C. PARADOX

D. LEADERSHIP

E. EVOLUTION

F. DEVELOPMENT

Figure 17: Essential elements for champion families to balance

Ignore any one of these elements at your peril, and be aware of the need to adjust and accommodate them.

It's an interplay between individual and collective. The family champion is an individual (or small number of individuals), but also part of a system that can nurture or impede their efforts.

Family champions deal in paradoxes. The most successful families, as supported in many cases by family champions, recognize that issues are not always *either-or* but are sometimes *both-and*. The family and business can grow from taking two seemingly opposed perspectives or holding two conflicting priorities at once, such as promoting *both* tradition *and* innovation.[14]

---

[14] For more on the challenge and benefits of paradox in family business, see Schuman, A., Stutz, S., & Ward, J.L. (2010). *Family business as paradox.* New York, NY: Palgrave Macmillan US.

Family champion provides dedicated leadership. Employee and champion are not mutually exclusive roles, but they are usually different people. In the families that have achieved great success, the role of family leadership is typically separate from business leadership. Each domain takes a serious investment of resources, and the distinct roles tend to require distinct skills.

Family champion might not even be a family member. In some cases, the *family* champion is a non-family trusted advisor. Such an advisor can play the role of catalyst because, in some family systems, a non-family member is more neutral and better able to move things forward.

It's about growth through evolution. Family champions and champion families evolve over time, learn from trial and error, take risks, and grow from experiences (even challenges and setbacks). They use missteps as learning opportunities and approach challenges constructively.

Consider the champion family a work in progress, rather than something with an end state or finish line. A champion family might be in any of several stages, with the goal of becoming even better.

Development is the cornerstone. Family champions and champion families focus sharply on individual and collective development. They seek out and take advantage of development opportunities for themselves and other family members.

Dealing in Paradox

We know a family champion who helped resolve the problem of inclusivity versus qualifications in governance roles. The family wanted members in governance roles, but also wanted high qualification standards for these positions. Erring on one side or the other would mean either too many unqualified family members in governance or a qualification bar so high it would eliminate most members. The champion promoted family consensus around increasing qualifications and expectations for different governance levels. They agreed:

- Small committees – most inclusive
- Family council – inclusive, but with greater qualifications and expectations
- Formal board of directors – the least inclusive, with a high degree of qualification and expectations

The collaborative process led to open discussion and the appointment of a wide range of qualified family members to governance roles.

Figure 18: Dealing in paradox

Questions to consider

- Each family champion has a unique origin story—what potential origin stories do you see developing in your family? How can you help facilitate the story for yourself or other possible champions in your family?
- We presented a list of characteristics family champions tend to have, including leadership, communication skills, commitment, and capacity. Where do you see these concentrated in your extended family, indicating a potential champion or champions?
- How could you develop further skills or capabilities to make you a greater asset to your family?
- Family champions and the families that house them work together for optimal results. We discussed many ways in which this interplay benefits the extended family. Take a look at the lists again and try to identify ways in which your family exemplifies a given quality or process.
- How could you improve the functioning of your own system and the interplay between (potential) family champions and the larger group? In what ways could you inspire others to take more of a role?

CHAPTER 5: DEVELOPING AND SUPPORTING CHAMPION FAMILIES

The importance of a Family Championship Plan

It's not easy to build a sustainable, thriving business family. It requires ongoing individual and group effort and a dynamic interplay of people and activities. But when family members grow into champion roles, the group gets better at identifying and addressing critical ownership issues together. And, ideally, a positive feedback cycle improves how they work as a team. Although champion families achieve their longevity through hard work and sustained action, their efforts are far from random. They employ thoughtful planning, road maps, and plans to guide them.

We have observed that strategic planning for the *family* is as important as strategic planning for the business. But how many families have a well-conceived, broadly communicated strategic plan for their ownership goals? The most successful business families plan for their future as owners. This forethought—in both vision and attention to detail— contributes directly to their engagement, achievement, and longevity. The plans are adaptable by design and they evolve as the family grows and changes. A well-conceived *Family Championship Plan* (FCP) enables the family to manage complexities and challenges with greater confidence and, ultimately, success.

This chapter highlights the elements that champion families build into their strategic plans, including the way they address relationships and entrepreneurship. It also outlines the process and potential pitfalls, along with an example plan.

CHAPTER 5

The Family Championship Plan

The FCP is a comprehensive, long-term plan that employs the seven traits of family championship to help family business owners determine:

- *where* they want to go
- *how* they are going to get there
- *what* they need to do to achieve their goals

Although the areas of focus are specific to each family, the overall aim is to help the family build its capabilities and skills to be the best ownership group it can be: to be stewards of the business, care for the family, and sustain their legacy. It's a process that can lead to becoming a true champion family.[15]

We emphasize championship as part of the plan's name because it points to the importance of a family's ability to care for the business and succeed as a family over time. It takes time, planning, and execution to develop the owners' understanding and capabilities. The FCP is an aspirational and strategic plan. It gives the family a road map for how to build themselves into a champion family through continuous and thoughtful improvement at the individual and group levels.

Before you begin

Our seven key elements of champion families provide structure and focus for an FCP: leadership, purpose, values, governance, education, communication, and relationships. But before you dive into creating a plan, we encourage you to assess where you currently stand on each element. Identify your areas of strength, but also the areas with greatest

---

[15] Others have suggested plans for family development, including the parallel planning process of Carlock, R.S., & Ward, J.L. (2010). *When family businesses are best: The parallel planning process for family harmony and business success*, Palgrave Macmillan US, discussed in earlier chapters. We see our family championship plan as an even more accessible approach with specific dimensions families can work on to improve their capabilities and impact across key areas.

opportunity for growth. Use your evaluation based on the seven elements as a starting place, then adapt into a rough plan that you can refine.

These points will help you define the scope of your work:

Goals are critical. Think carefully about the big-picture goals for your work. What can you accomplish in the next year? Where would you like to be in three to five years? Setting goals can add structure and accountability to your process. These progress-markers can be always be refined, and they keep you on track. As you begin to formulate your plan, articulate some specific goals you want to meet, along with a rough timeline for accomplishing them.

The goals you choose will vary. Some relate specifically to the *business*, and others might be more *interpersonal* in nature. Goals provide the family a chance to specify accomplishments they want, and they serve as checkpoints along the way to keep things moving.

It's a continuum. As you consider your FCP, don't think in terms of a finish line for your goals. Elements of your plan vary in intensity, but they might be ongoing. Consider tracking your progress on a continuum, with focus on areas where you need the most development. For those areas where you're more advanced, how do you sustain your gains? Assess your capabilities in each area and focus your energy and attention. You might also think in terms of cycles of work. To create and carry out a plan like this, you'll need a long-term effort. Be prepared for alternating periods of intense work and relative quiet. If you anticipate the cyclical nature of this progress, you'll be better able to manage expectations.

Collaboration required. Creating a championship plan is a significant undertaking, well beyond the scope of what one person can do. We have observed that small teams are most effective in creating this road map, with consistent feedback and input from the family. So you might want to convene a small committee or group of people who can invest the needed time. This group can meet with the larger family ownership group at specific intervals to gather input, solicit feedback, and maintain accountability. Also, think of creating and enacting the FCP as running a marathon relay race. You need many people handing off the baton to one another to make it happen. When one person gets tired, make sure the next person is ready to engage and able to keep running in the right direction. Different people have different interests, so get people involved in what excites them most.

Key elements of a Family Championship Plan

The components of your FCP are based on the seven characteristics of champion families presented in Chapter 3. This section reviews them, with questions to think about as you develop your FCP. In accordance with your own unique needs, place them in any order that makes sense to you... or even add elements of your own.

The next section details the elements of an FCP, along with questions to guide you in applying these elements to your needs.

Leadership

Champion families function best when the leaders are in positions that match their capabilities. Leaders must have dedication and willingness to work hard in order to be successful. With that in mind, who comes to mind? Who are the people you can develop as leaders? Putting together a plan for leadership is a critical part of building continuity as a champion family. Outline steps to identify, develop, and support your current and future leaders. Make this a collaborative process—involve the family and these leaders in formulating the plan. Consider who your current leaders are, who your high-potential leadership candidates are, and how they may be developed.

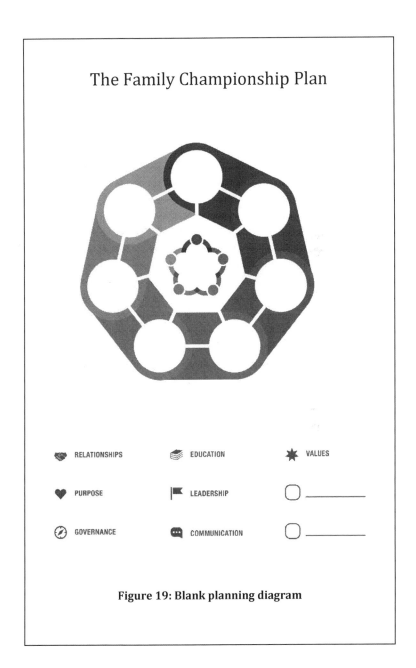

The Family Championship Plan

RELATIONSHIPS   EDUCATION   VALUES

PURPOSE   LEADERSHIP

GOVERNANCE   COMMUNICATION

Figure 19: Blank planning diagram

Purpose

Chapter 3 emphasized that purpose is tied closely to collective vision. What is the biggest vision for your family's ownership of the enterprise? The *big vision* provides an aspirational goal for the family legacy. It is large and compelling enough to stretch across—and motivate—subsequent generations. Vision development is thus critical to the FCP, and is something that fosters family championship.

For example, in a family champion example earlier in the book, third-generation member Carla helped her family develop their True North Story at a family retreat. As hoped, the vision became something the whole family could aim for and aspire to. The fair, inclusive, and thoughtful process of getting to this vision also contributed to buy-in from the entire family.

Families have to know where they want to go as a group, and the *big vision* serves as the foundation for legacy-building. Compelling vision statements can be nice shorthand for what the family aspires to collectively.

Values

Most families have a good intuitive sense of their values, but are those values clearly articulated? Craig Aronoff and John Ward (pg. 8, 2001)[16] wrote that values *lay the bedrock for culture* and guide decision-making. We see the effort to develop and define values as an important piece of being a champion family and building your FCP. A values-identification project can be an enjoyable way to align the family around what you collectively believe is most important.

---

[16] Aronoff, C.E., & Ward, J.L. (2011). *Family business values: How to assure a legacy of continuity and success.* New York, NY: Palgrave Macmillan US.

Reed Family Vision

The Reed family took a democratic approach to determining the future of their business:

The Reed Family Vision Statement

The Reed Family, by having integrity in all actions, believing in the virtue of hard work, philanthropic leadership, and preserving family values, seeks to achieve the enhancement of generational unity and growth by means of:

Owning and operating businesses that instill a forward-thinking workplace culture where people want to work and customers find it easy to do business,

Preserving and enhancing:

- Intellectual capital
- Emotional capital
- Financial capital
- Entrepreneurial culture

Therefore, as the owners, we direct the Board to:

- Optimize the realization of the premium value of the business enterprise.
- Provide an annual dividend from after tax earnings while maintaining conservative monetary practices.
- Actively seek other commercial endeavors for the family to invest.
- Continue to develop and grow current product lines while retaining product relevance in the market place.
- Empower the management team to plan for the future of the company's growth.

Figure 20: Reed family vision

Through various exercises, an outside resource can help your family consolidate your values and translate them into an actionable form.

Governance

The primary structures and forums (that help the family to organize, make decisions, and communicate with the business) are the Family Council and Board of Directors. Some families have a separate ownership council, along with smaller committee groups or task forces. Almost every champion family we have seen has these structures, or at least equivalent ways to make decisions together. In a family that does not have these in place, the FCP probably includes their formation as a high-priority central element. If these governance structures already exist, the FCP is likely to focus on how to make them even better. The result might be to broaden the engagement or membership of an existing family council or add independent directors to a previously all-family board of directors.

Most governance forums take time to become effective, regardless of the family's intent and baseline capability. The more thought you place into the membership, purpose, and communication processes for governance, the more valuable it can be. Think about what structures would help you make the best decisions, consider where you want your governance to be, and then map the practical steps to put those changes in place.

Education

Aspiring champion families need to navigate the challenging waters where business and family meet. An entire field has emerged to guide you through this complexity, with a range of offerings (and prices). Educational resources can be incredibly valuable for helping the family integrate knowledge and stimulate thinking about how to manage their unique situation and thrive. FCP-related plans for education can simple, such as sharing research-based or practical articles to discuss together. Or it can be as far-reaching as complete educational programs with full curricula and well-designed courses, conducted either in-house or by an

---

Education topics for business families

- Business skills or aptitude (with emphasis on the family's specific business areas)
  - Family ownership 101
  - Legal issues
- Financial knowledge
  - Understanding financial statements
  - Taxes and estate planning
  - Wealth management
  - Trustee and beneficiary relationships
- History
  - Business (key events and decisions)
  - Family (key members and events)
- Governance (purpose and operation of boards and other structures, how to choose and evaluate board members, and so on)
- Leadership skills
  - Communication (among all three circles: family, owners, business managers)
  - Ins and outs of in-laws (such as onboarding and off-boarding spouses and understanding their role in business and governance)
  - Building the most effective culture
- Case studies of other family businesses

Figure 21: Education topics

outside party. Educational programs often integrate multiple sources including articles, books, speakers, workshops, conferences, consultants, and internal family resources. Figure 21 includes the main areas where educational resources can be of value (see the Appendix for a list of resources).[17]

Communication

Perhaps the most important aspect of successful champion families is how they communicate. Communication is the foundation of any successful group, including business families who have to manage both family dynamics and business responsibilities. Every successful champion family we have worked with has effective communication practices. This critical capability is not something that champion families leave to chance. Instead, they actively address their communication, ensuring common language, guidelines, and structured ways to address conflict.

The term *effective communication* is hard to define precisely, but we see several shared features of communication in champion families. Champion families are able to consistently be *honest* and *authentic* with one another, and to share their views in a way that is *respectful*. These families can disagree with one another in a constructive manner and incorporate multiple viewpoints into their decision-making. Communication is open and forthright, and people can take one another at face value. There is little second-guessing at hidden meanings. These healthy communication styles interact with healthy relationships in beneficial feedback cycles. See Figure 22 for more on this critical area.

---

[17] For an especially helpful resource on education in family business, see Schuman, A., & Ward, J.L. (2011). *Family education for business-owning families: Strengthening bonds by learning together.* New York, NY: Palgrave Macmillan US.

Consider how you might build the communication culture in your family as part of your plan. Where are your communication patterns strong and healthy? Where do you struggle with communication? In this area, outside resources can be especially helpful to educate your family.

A consultant, psychologist, or facilitated workshop can shine a light on existing communication styles and bring in new information. And an outside facilitator can do it without any of the history or family relationship issues you might have. Specialists and seminars can bring new insight on topics such as non-violent communication, crucial conversations, or *fierce conversations*. These techniques can be effective as you develop a foundation of skills and support a culture of respectful, supportive communication.

Bring out the elephant-in-the-room

Families are often unwilling to talk about sensitive or conflict-inducing topics. The awkwardness and reluctance around these issues can impede development or even derail it. We encourage the families we work with to discuss these uncomfortable topics in a structured setting, ideally with the help of an experienced outside advisor. For example, one family we know schedules an Elephant-in-the-Room session at their annual retreats to talk about things they normally might not talk about in an open forum. Individual members can submit touchy topics to the advisor beforehand, to make them easier to bring up.

Example topics include the implications of marriage (new family members) or divorce (lost family members), ownership issues, and ongoing, disruptive conflicts among members or branches.

Figure 22: Elephant in the room

Relationships

Relationships form the foundation that holds everything together in business families. Nothing we describe here is relevant or useful if the family members involved do not enjoy being together. Take stock of the relationships in your family and note your energy around this topic. Do you like gathering as a family? Are family meetings sources of energy... or dread?

Regardless of your current state, investing in relationships is a vital, ongoing aspect of sustaining a champion family. Consider relationships as they relate to the business and to the family. You interact with one another in a variety of ways—as business and family, as siblings, uncles, aunts, cousins. We believe that relationships grow when tested in healthy ways, and that shared experience creates friendship.

You can facilitate relationships in many ways. For example, family meetings don't have to be all business. They can include social events to ensure that the family knows one another not only in the meeting room, but in more informal settings. One business-owning family has a tradition of going bowling as part of family meetings. It's an enjoyable way to interact and relax, engage in some healthy competition, and forge critical bonds and communication. Or you could plan a facilitated team-building retreat for owners. Another family we know has a water-focused business, so they planned a dual-purpose experiential trip: They toured a water treatment plant they are building and discussed the business-related aspects of the project, and then they went on a family river trip together on the same water. It was fun, a relationship-building experience they still talk about today.

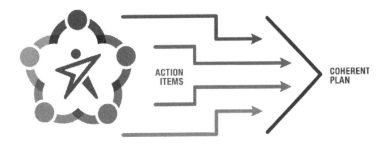

Figure 23: Turn action items into a plan

Now what? Carrying out the FCP

Let's say you've done some assessment of your family's progress, and have created an FCP. Maybe it was even easier than you thought. But now you have to bring the plan into action. Not so easy. To do this right, we recommend that you prioritize and assess your resources, using these questions:

- What are the most important tasks to accomplish first?
- Where can you make tangible progress most easily and feel as if you're moving forward?
- How many people do you have available to work on individual projects?
- Which projects are short-term and accomplishable, and which ones are more long-term in scope?

Use these questions to build structure into the plan, and *don't* try to tackle everything at once. Make small gains and build on your accomplishments. You will probably have to create a *plan for the plan*, or a map and timeline for projects. Be sure to make it realistic. Remember: Almost everything will take more time than you think!

The FCP as a foundation for continuity

The FCP promotes a true foundation for continuity of both the family and business. In a 2016 book, our colleague and fellow family business advisor David Lansky lays out five pillars of the foundation for family enterprise continuity of wealth and relationships. Your work on the seven key elements of family championship through a thoughtful FCP aligns well with these pillars. Lansky's foundation includes:[18]

Learning capacity: The family's ability to learn new information or practices and communicate them across the three circles of family enterprise: family, ownership, business. This capacity helps the family adapt to changing circumstances within and outside the family. The education and communication elements of the FCP support this pillar.

Family-ness: A sense of caring and intimacy among members. Family-ness is present when members enjoy spending time with one another and share healthy levels of trust. This quality helps families take risks together, such as having difficult conversations about relationships or expectations. Relationships and communication are critical to family-ness.

Safe communication culture: An atmosphere built on formal and informal opportunities to discuss important issues including relationships, overall comfort with two-way dialogue, and a willingness to voice personal responsibility for conflicts, failures, or other difficult circumstances. All FCP elements should be aimed at promoting such an environment.

Commitment to personal development: Family emphasis on improving individual members' financial and legal literacy, emotional intelligence, and general well-being through education and other means. This commitment enables individuals to contribute to group welfare more effectively.

---

[18] Lansky, D. (2016). Family wealth continuity: Building a foundation for the future. New York, NY: Palgrave MacMillan US.

Effective leadership of change: Individuals and groups are willing to step into leadership roles as related to ownership and business issues, including developing a meaningful vision for the family's future based on its identified collective purpose.

The Andersons' Family Championship Plan

In Chapter 3 we met the Andersons, a third-generation Midwestern US family with businesses in architecture, construction, and real estate. The second-generation siblings run the firm, with advice from their founder parents. Two second-generation in-laws also work in the business, and several third-generation members have completed internships or part-time work within the enterprise and are interested in future roles in both the business and its governance. Recently the family formed a continuity committee, including outside advisors, to develop a plan for ownership and leadership succession. In this section we present more details about how they developed this plan for the future, reflecting many elements of an FCP (though they didn't formally call it that). Every family does not have strength in every element of family championship. The Andersons are typical, with a varied profile across the seven areas.

The Andersons were motivated to develop a plan by the family CEO's interest in shifting from an operating to a governance role in the intermediate term, requiring attention to ownership and leadership succession. Their early work highlighted the need for a more comprehensive plan that included a clear purpose and vision. They needed something the broad ownership group could focus on, along with supporting elements related to succession, governance, operating agreements, estate plans, and branch representation. "We wanted to develop something everyone would be excited about being part of," the CEO said.

The family took a structured approach, ensuring broad participation as well as generational and branch representation by multiple members, regular meetings and task force work, and the help of outside advisors. Through this process the family agreed on a Big Vision they called *Moving Forward, Giving Back*, highlighting their broad purpose as a business-owning family.

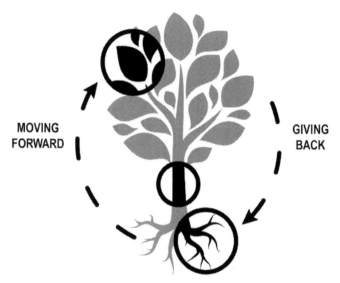

MOVING
FORWARD

GIVING
BACK

Figure 24: Moving forward, giving back

The *moving forward* component represented how they could advance their knowledge and interests as owners, at both the individual and group levels, for the good of the enterprise, future generations, and themselves. The *giving back* element reflected the founder's values in supporting individual family members and their community.

The moving forward part of the plan contained multiple elements, including focused work on *governance*. Thus the plan included clear goals and a timeline for creating an advisory board with outside advisors that would evolve into a fiduciary board with independent directors. Another element of this part of the plan was an emphasis on personal development through *education*. They wanted to help individual members identify their interests—whether related to the family enterprise or not—and to pursue these in meaningful ways, including formal and informal education. The idea was to both build individual members' skills and position those interested for *leadership* within the enterprise, whether for the business, family, or both.

Another moving forward element focused on promoting family harmony by fostering *communication and relationships*. Although the Anderson siblings lived close to one another, several members of the third generation had moved away from their hometown, and others were sure to follow. So the family emphasized regular family reunions (including holidays and special events such as graduations) and team-building activities (such as a mountain ropes course and group hikes), to promote bonding and communication. This element also included development of a clear conflict resolution policy that stipulated members should try to work out issues among themselves first, and then to escalate as needed to an impartial party within or outside the family. The Andersons believed they got along well as an extended family, but wanted to use this element and the broader vision to avoid buildup of resentments at the generational, branch, or individual levels.

For the giving back part of the FCP, the family focused on supporting individual members and the broader local and regional community. For example, they agreed to commit funds to a family bank that could provide financial support for the personal development goals individuals identified as part of the moving forward component. This included diverse activities ranging from paying for travel (to and lessons at a famous music institute for a young third-generation member who showed significant promise as a violinist), to funding several older third-generation members' attendance at a week-long seminar on family enterprise governance at an out-of-state university. The bank could also be used to support family members' approved business ventures.

For the philanthropic part of the FCP, which spoke to the founder's values and the family's broad purpose, the family agreed to set giving goals for amounts dedicated to community charities and other social initiatives, and to develop a clear approval process for identifying worthy causes. The founder had previously set loose guidelines for giving (and influenced strongly where any grants went). The family realized they wanted a selection system that focused giving more strategically on specific areas (such as education and the environment) while still taking into account branch and individual philanthropic preferences.

The process for developing the FCP was just as important as its outputs, and it included regular meetings, task force work, and active facilitation by family members and outside advisors. For example, Rory, the younger second-generation sister and evolving family champion, led key segments of the meetings, including those focused on personal development and creation of a system for conflict resolution. The family brought in an outside expert on governance to discuss their board-related goals at several meetings. They also developed an Anderson Family Code of Conduct that extended to behavior within and outside these meetings and emphasized upholding values including respect, trust, communication, integrity, and integration. Finally, the family used practices such as taking frequent breaks during discussions to prevent fatigue, passing a *talking stick* that prevented interruptions, and elephant-in-the-room sessions to speak about uncomfortable but important topics (see Figure 22).

"There were times when it felt overwhelming to take on as much as we did," Rory Anderson said, "but all the work was worth it because we came out with a clear plan for the future and a better understanding of what everyone wanted." The family recognized that their plan was not a static document but an evolving blueprint for how to work together across several areas as a cohesive family united by a big vision for their future, with an emphasis on continuous improvement.

Practices for Creating FCPs

The Andersons exemplified several excellent practices for creating FCPs. They examined their current situation, set priorities, identified action steps, and specified milestones toward the goals they had determined for their family business.

Figure 25: Timeline and milestones

Keep these practices in mind as you begin to develop your FCP:

Remember the purpose. It is important to know *why* you and your family are creating an FCP. It's not just an exercise, and it needs to be intentional in nature. How the FCP process and output serve your broader goals as a business-owning family must be clear to everyone.

Appreciate the process. We believe that in most family development work, the *journey* is at least as important as the destination. So the process of developing an FCP is as important as its outcome—and more important in many cases, since the outcome should evolve. As the Anderson example demonstrates, key elements of process include (1) *group effort* that allows more to get done and is adequately representative of the broader family; (2) principles of *fair process* to guide the work; (3) *structure and regularity* (such as regular meetings) to make sure the work gets done and that people don't lose interest or momentum; and (4) *healthy communication and relationships,* even at the expense of some other elements, to ensure ongoing trust and family cohesion.

Communicate. We've emphasized communication several times in this book, and it bears repeating. Being able to communicate effectively as a family is foundational to many processes, and an effective FCP can emerge only from a collaborative process with good communication. The process of building the FCP can be used to help develop communication, but it's ideal to start with a strong communication base, make adjustments and refinements along the way, and have regular check-ins.

Facilitate. Family members, especially family champions, can help facilitate the FCP process, but family business consultants and professional facilitators can be valuable resources as well. They can help ask interesting questions, mediate the speaking time, synthesize key ideas and insights, coax out the elephants-in-the-room, and manage the process objectively, with no personal agenda. A neutral professional acts on behalf of the entire group and can help keep things on track. The Andersons used both family-based and outside facilitators with good results.

Make it comprehensive, yet simple. The FCP must be comprehensive enough to address the complexities involved in being a business family, but simple enough to understand and be actionable. Achieving this balance might seem daunting at first, but it is both manageable and realistic. Start small, because you can always build on the plan. Don't be so far-reaching in scope that the plan is unwieldy and difficult to put into action (see Pitfalls section). The plan need not be perfect, but it has to be good enough to mean something to the family and guide their actions. Simple themes and organizing principles also go a long way, as suggested by the Andersons' Moving Forward, Giving Back concept.

Integrate. Aim the FCP at *synthesizing* multiple viewpoints and components for how to be the best business-owing family possible. A plan of this nature is far-reaching and often requires engagement from diverse family members, board members, key employees, and trusted advisors. Gather and incorporate ideas and viewpoints from the broad family to create a plan the entire group can embrace. Another important aspect of being integrative is to appreciate and understand the systemic nature of being a business family. The actions of one part of the system, such as a given generation, branch, or member, affect all other components. An effective FCP takes into account the integration of the multiple sub-systems in an enterprising family at the levels of ideas, interests, and capabilities.

Keep it practical. The FCP must include concrete, practical steps to achieve goals, along with a timeline showing specific milestones and deadlines for many of them. Think about *how* to develop governance, *how* to become more effective owners, *what* type of education and skills are needed (governance, wealth management, communication, and others), and *how* to build or secure these.

Adapt. Just as families grow, evolve, and change, so must the FCP. The plan needs to allow for a natural adaptation to the needs of the family over time. The family must agree that the plan is not carved in stone by one generation. To support the growth of the plan, you can revisit it at regular intervals and integrate the perspectives of the rising generation. These younger members can contribute a fresh generational and cultural voice that adds to the plan in important ways.

Plan for the future. It takes time to develop and implement plans of this ambitious scope. Remember to move at a pace that is realistic. Plan for a long-term investment of time and energy into not only creating the plan, but also in seeing it put into action. Sustainability is a crucial element in building a strategy that produces meaningful outcomes.

CHAPTER 5

Pitfalls of developing an FCP

Finally, it's important to be wary of potential pitfalls, roadblocks, or traps related to the FCP development process. Here are several we've observed:

Taking on too much. As the Anderson example suggests, it might feel as if you've taken on too much when you first work on a FCP. This feeling can lead to loss of momentum or even a stalled process. Try to assess what the family is ready to handle *now*, and save some items for later if necessary. Aim for slow and steady progress that emphasizes broad, long-term involvement and sustainable action.

Underinvestment in the process or plan. Just as it's important to invest sufficient participation in the FCP development work, it might be important to make investments in other resources. For example, you might need to incur meeting space fees, books, outside advisors, or other expenses. Underinvestment of time and energy can happen at any point where participants are either stretched too thin or lack the commitment to engage. Gauge member commitment and invest in the resources needed to develop a plan people want to execute.

Branchism. A common issue among multigenerational business families, *branchism* refers to a tendency for family branches to exhibit an us-versus-them mentality. In building an FCP, branchism prevents adequate investment and will likely derail the process entirely. The effort cannot succeed if family branches compete to uphold their own interests. Assess and address potential threats *before* initiating more formal FCP development work.

The FCP can serve as the backbone of your family efforts to build your legacy. Investing in the plan is a worthwhile endeavor and provides a roadmap for current and future success. In the next chapter, we show you how to start the process of fostering championship at the individual and group levels.

Questions to consider

- Based on what you read in the chapter, what does the concept of a Family Championship Plan mean to you? What are your hopes and fears related to developing an FCP for your family?
- Think about the seven components that make up any FCP. What components do you believe your family can develop more expediently and why? What elements may be more challenging? Why?
- Relationships and communication form the foundation for an effective FCP. What are your family's strengths in this area? Weaknesses? What elephant-in-the-room issues (unspoken conflicts or awkward subjects) might exist and how might you address these in a healthy way?
- The process of creating an FCP is as important as the outcome. What evidence do you have for your family's strengths or weaknesses in carrying out important, larger-scale processes? What steps can you take to improve?
- We presented a list of pitfalls that might impede family development as related to an FCP or otherwise, including overextension, underinvestment, and branchism. Which of these is your family most susceptible to? Why, and what solutions might be feasible?

CHAPTER 6: TAKE THESE IDEAS INTO ACTION

How to move forward

We have presented many interrelated ideas in this book about family champions and champion families, including their origins, dynamics, interplay, and how to foster their growth and development at individual and group levels. In this chapter, rather than repeating or summarizing material presented earlier, we want to offer practical tips for moving forward with championship efforts, ways of thinking about the ideas here as you progress, and potential obstacles along the way.

We believe that trying to understand and implement the concepts here should feel like part of a *fun and inspiring* process. After all, you are investing in your individual development and your family's development. With that in mind, we encourage you to *start where you are*. Take stock of your current situation as a family, the resources you have, and the goals you want to reach. There is no wrong answer to "Where are you currently?" or "How do you feel about these ideas?" You have to work with the situation and resources that you have.

Families situations are all different. You might have a family champion in your family already (maybe it's you!). You might be saying to yourself, "That role sounds really intriguing for me or someone I know." You might believe your family fits the picture of a champion family in many respects already. Maybe you've have seen champion families accomplish a great deal and you're eager and inspired to implement similar practices to achieve your family's goals. Some readers will be inspired to action within their own family by the ideas in this book. But perhaps you're intimidated by the thought of trying to become a champion family because it seems too much of a stretch from your current situation.

Every great champion family had to start somewhere. Remember: A journey of a thousand miles begins with one step, as Lao Tzu wrote in the *Tao Te Ching*, and this is particularly true for business families.

> Small changes can lead to big transformations and, while there are no guaranteed outcomes, the only thing for certain is that failing to start the journey means ***you're already at your destination.***

The critical thing to keep in mind is that you have to adjust the roles of the family champion and the goals of champion families described here based on the specifics of *your* family's situation. Don't aim for exactly what we've presented or set your expectations to match what you've seen in other families. The ideas in this chapter help you to apply the concepts and advice in this book to your family in your situation, transforming good ideas and intentions into real action and sustainable change.

Where are you now? Where do you want to go?

A good place to start any meaningful process is with meaningful questions. Asking good questions can help you understand where you are, where you want to go, and possible routes you might take to get there. First, refer back to the questions we asked at the end of each chapter. In this section, we also offer some starter questions to help you gather important information about your family's current situation, goals, and resources. You can answer these questions yourself, but also consider gathering answers from others including family leaders, family owners who don't work in the business, and board members. Then look for places of convergence, alignment, and inspiration to build momentum based on your common ground. Also notice areas of ambiguity and divergence, and then think about how to address these areas of potential growth in a constructive manner.

Family champion questions

- If we don't have a specific goal or vision, or if people disagree on what these should be, what can I do to start the conversation that would lead to one?
- What do I want our legacy to be? What do others want our legacy to be and how can I help develop a unified vision?
- How can I contribute to the family in different areas as an owner?
- What do I need to learn in order to contribute in the best way possible?
- What champion elements or potential do I see in myself or other individual family members?

Champion family questions

- What is our goal and vision as a family? Do we even have one?
- How close are we to achieving this goal? What are the major obstacles we face?
- What are our biggest opportunities as a family?
- What are our biggest challenges?
- What are the priorities for starting or continuing our work?
- How can we involve the most people in our development process?
- What champion elements or potential do I see in our family?

We encourage you to answer these questions in a thoughtful manner. Write down your answers. Ask other engaged family members the same questions. Begin to interact with the questions and answers in a way that moves you forward—even if it doesn't feel like that's where you're going.

What you can do now

In this section we present some basic actions to take *right now* to work toward creating an environment that supports family champions and champion families and their interplay. Use the questions in the previous section and incorporate the ideas that emerge. These ideas are meant to get you thinking, and they are designed to apply to families in many situations. As always, adapt and apply them in the way that's most useful for you.

Action item: Develop family champions

One of the most important aspects of family champions is the motivation and desire to do the work necessary to emerge as a leader. So we believe that this is the starting place: Who has the motivation, desire, energy, and vision to take on the challenging and rewarding work of acting as a catalyst in your family system? If that person is you, congratulations! We encourage you to keep going and to transition from interest to action. If it's someone else, think about how to inspire and prompt that person into taking on a more significant role, and remember, this might take months or years.

Ultimately, how to move forward will depend on *who* you are within the broad family system, so let's look at that next.

Younger family members

If you're a young family member and you've been inspired by this talk of family champions, here are some things to do:

- Become a *student* of family businesses. Read as much as you can, and use our book list as a starting place.
- See if you can attend one of the many *conferences or seminars* about being a business family.
- Take a leadership or communication course.
- Start *speaking up, start asking questions*, including those inspired by this book. Of course, do this in a way that is respectful and constructive. Stirring the pot can be helpful, but the family has to be able to integrate new energy.
- Connect with other family champions to learn of their experiences.

Older family members

If you're an *older-generation member* and like the idea of developing a family champion to help move your family into the future, here are some things to do:

- *Identify potential family champions* and think about how to encourage their contributions.
- *Invite these people* to take on a more significant role. Ask them questions and make them feel appreciated for their views.
- Sometimes you have to *create space* in order for someone else to flourish. You (or another older-generation family member) might have to step back—whether from formal or informal roles—to enable someone else to step forward.
- *Place potential family champions in positions of responsibility*, to help them build critical credibility and trust. Support them in their actions.

- *Accept change.* Don't be afraid of new people and new ideas. Create the conditions that allow both tradition and innovation to work together.
- *Invest in education.* Invite the family to attend a conference together. Give your family champion the opportunities to learn and shine.

Non-family professionals

If you're a professional (advisor, accountant, lawyer, banker, and so on) working with a family, here's where to start:

- *Understand the nuances of family dynamics.* Just because you see someone who would be a good family champion does not mean the family sees that person in the same way.
- If there are clear family champions, *breathe life into their actions.* Support them, challenge them, and help them to be even better and more influential at what they do.
- *Work on behalf of the entire system.* Remember, a family champion is always part of a system, and aligning too much with one person can alienate other people.
- *Resource the family.* Help the family build their own resources. Avoid giving them easy answers or formulaic solutions that do not stick. Champion families stand on their own feet and tend to use professional advisors to help them move past specific hurdles, not in perpetuity.

Action item: Create a Family Championship Plan to become a *champion family*

As we emphasized in the previous chapter, creating a Family Championship Plan is a long process and broad engagement by the family across the seven core elements is vital. We also recognize that if you're reading this book, you might be motivated to begin a project like this.

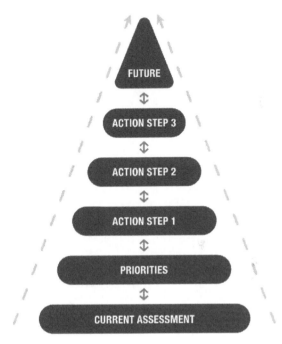

Figure 26: One step at a time

Current assessment—where are we now?

The first step is to answer the "Where are we now?" question. The assessment of your current situation guides everything that happens next. As you thoroughly evaluate where you are, your priorities emerge. Those priorities dictate the action steps you need to take in order to achieve your vision, and so on.

Approach this potentially formidable task in manageable pieces. In the first step, you create a vision that all family members accept and rally around. The vision gives you a goal to strive for, a True North, as described in our example of the family champion Carla the Coach. You might need to spend some dedicated time gathering as a family to decide what your vision even is.

Figure 19 in Chapter 5 shows a blank diagram you can use to place the seven key elements in an order that fits your situation and to add elements, if necessary. Reviewing the key elements, ask these questions:

- *Leadership:* Who are current leaders in the family and how are they performing? Who are strong potential future leaders and how might they be developed?
- *Purpose or Vision:* What do we see as our purpose as a business family? What vision serves this purpose best? What does being a champion family look like for us?
- *Values:* What are our values as a family? Can we articulate them and understand how they influence our decisions and actions across domains?
- *Governance:* What governance structures are in place for the business and the family? If these are in place, what do we need to do to make them better? If we have none, what are the most effective councils to support both the family and the business?
- *Education:* What are the most important topics we need to learn more about as individuals and as a business family? How can we access the right resources to learn this?
- *Communication:* How do we communicate today, among individuals and groups (families, branches, generations)? What do we need to do to improve our communication as a group?
- *Relationships:* Do we have strong relationships across the extended family? Have we crafted a comprehensive code of conduct for how we interact as a business family? How can we strengthen our relationships in general?

Priorities—What is most important?

- What is our current status for each of these areas?
- Which of these areas need the most immediate attention from us as a family in order to achieve our goals?
- What's our first priority?

Action steps—What's next?

- Within each area, what can we do now?
- What can we plan for in the future?
- What is the ideal outcome of working on these areas— overall and within each?
- What is one tangible step that I can do to make progress in the highest-priority areas?
- What can I ask others to do?

For each of these areas, think about building a project template for advancing the initiative. Start where you are, think of the end goal, and begin to map out the steps needed to get there. We fully recognize the challenge of engaging in a project of this magnitude. Some families are capable of doing this work largely on their own, but others might need to enlist a professional to help get them started and keep them on track. Creating a FCP takes work, and we believe that the investment is well worth the time.

Common mistakes

Moving toward championship as an individual or family is not easy. It takes a lot of commitment, planning, and action, and it all takes place over a long period of time. As part of your approach, keep in mind the mistakes we've observed in our work with many different families. You can benefit from their experiences, learn from these mistakes and prevent them from happening in your journey toward success. Refer to the even more specific list of FCP pitfalls in the previous chapter as well.

Short-termism: Too often, families get excited about their potential for change, sparked by attending a conference on family business, reading a book about family enterprise, or having a conversation with an advisor or fellow family business member. They take some initial action, such as calling a meeting or presenting an idea, but then nothing much happens and the family gets frustrated and loses motivation. They expected immediate, short-term results.

Real change of any kind requires a long-term view. To make big changes, you have to think *small* at first. What are the small early steps you can take, as an individual or a group, to start working toward bigger change? Use the ideas here to work on both ends: developing a vision for the family, and then taking the small early steps to get there. Keep in mind that change should be measured in years, not quarters.

Sprinting too fast: As a corollary to short-termism, be aware that some individuals and families get so excited about their new ideas and initiatives that they try to do too much too soon. Everyone is enthusiastic, but they try to tackle every project at the same time. They quickly discover that they cannot accomplish anything. It is much better to create small successes that you can build on. Family business success is a marathon, not a sprint.

The danger of over-functioning: Sometimes the family champion does such a good job of promoting initial change—whether driven by passion, personality, or both—that it relieves the broader family of the need to learn and act. Or a small group takes on the lion's share of the work, enabling others to enjoy a free ride. Although unintentional, this kind of super achievement stunts family growth and is not ideal in the long run. It places too much responsibility on one person or a small group, even if they're willing to take it on. In some cases, the champion needs to pull back and lead from behind in order to help others develop. One family champion we know, for example, chose not to accept the family council chair role and encouraged another member to take it on... specifically to spread leadership throughout the system.

Getting out too far ahead: This is related to over-functioning. Sometimes, in a rush to drive change, an individual or small group sprints ahead of the family, leaving others behind or uninvolved. A family champion might say, "We need a fiduciary board with independents—now," when the family has not even considered forming an advisory board yet. The idea is to move at the pace that makes sense for your family and to bring people along as they are ready. This might involve some coaxing and urging, but that's fine and even expected. So try to work to bring everyone along where possible, making it a group run rather than a solo dash.

Right role, wrong person: Some leader-types are successful in other pursuits, but the wrong choice to act as a family champion or lead a given initiative within an FCP. An effective family champion or other leader not only needs basic commitment as well as communication and interpersonal skills, but also *credibility* within the family—and alignment with the family's culture and values. We think it's especially important to have a champion who acts as a *servant leader*, working to improve the capacity and capability of the entire family. Ideal family champions often lead from behind, rather than just trying to get things done or improving their own skills.

There's a reason we call these people *family* champions. They need to live up to this role by considering the collective good. And remember that a family's current situation might also call for a one specific type of champion, but things change. Later developments might call for someone with a different skill-set or perspective.

Commit to continuous growth

We hope we've emphasized that acting as a family champion or champion family is not a time-limited role or event but an always-evolving process. There is vision, of course, but no final destination, because each family generation or phase will have different visions and goals, capabilities, and paths to reaching their objectives. While there's no secret formula for long-term success, there are specific things you can do to drive continuous growth and development. These include assessing carefully what's working and what isn't, making necessary adjustments regularly, celebrating victories large and small, (while also looking ahead to the next challenge), developing a fair process for decision-making, and creating family-related policies and practices.

Use this book in the way that works best for you and your family or one you advise, recognizing that championship is a process, not an endpoint. Don't wait for someone else to do it. Start where you are, commit, and engage others early and as fully as possible to join you on this rewarding journey. We commend you on your interest in building your business family, and we wish you the best on your journey toward collective success.

Question to consider

Each of the previous chapters has ended with a list of questions to consider, based on the chapter contents. This final chapter offers many actionable questions within the previous text itself, so we'll end with just one:

Are you ready to move toward family championship?

————◀●▶————

APPENDIX

You might find these resources helpful as you build your champion family.

Education

- *The Family Business Consulting Group*: Provides a wide range of educational materials including events, newsletters, books and free webinars dedicated to helping family businesses proper across generations. https://www.thefbcg.com/publications/

- *Business Families Foundation*: A not-for-profit charitable organization established to support, help and empower business families to ensure their sustainability and harmony for generations to come. http://www.businessfamilies.org/en/

- *Campden Events* (A division of Campden Wealth): Offers a variety of courses and retreats in international locations for family businesses. Subjects include family wealth, family business matters, and family office topics. http://www.campdenconferences.com

- *Center for Creative Leadership* (CCL): A highly regarded leadership development organization that uses structure and peer accountability to build leaders. Not a family business specific organization, but still highly applicable to family champions. http://www.ccl.org

- *Family Business Network International:* A global non-profit organization of business families. Headquartered in Lausanne, Switzerland; shares best practice and knowledge and offers an annual Summit. http://www.fbn-i.org

- *Family Business Alliance*: Based in Grand Rapids, MI, hosting a variety of events about family business topics, seminars, and speakers. http://www.fbagr.org

APPENDIX

- *Harvard Business School's Families in Business*: This leadership development program helps formulate strategies for critical issues, such as management succession, ownership control, and shareholder relationships. https://www.exed.hbs.edu

- *INSEAD*: An international business school based in Fontainebleau, France. Offers a variety of family business specific courses in entrepreneurship and leadership. http://www.insead.edu

- *Kellogg Executive Education* programs at Northwestern University: A variety of high quality programs designed for a deeper exploration of specific topics such as leadership and governance. http://www.kellogg.northwestern.edu/executive-education/individual-programs/executive-programs/fambiz.aspx

- *Transitions Conference*: Employs a panel and breakout format with all family speakers in a friendly, networking-oriented environment. Offered twice a year in the eastern and western United States. *Transitions* is a great introduction to family business concepts. http://www.familybusinessmagazine.com.

- *Young Presidents Organization (YPO)*: Offers an increasing focus on family businesses and hosts a YPO family business retreat annually, aimed at business leaders and their families. http://www.ypo.org

Periodicals

Bariso, J. (2016). This single question will tell you what you need to know about emotional intelligence. Inc. Magazine, October 3, 2016. Retrieved from http://www.inc.com/justin-bariso/this-single-question-will-tell-you-what-you-need-to-know-about-emotional-intelli.html

Tagiuri, R., & Davis, J. (1996). Bivalent attributes of a family firm. Family Business Review, 9(2), Summer 1996.

Vernon, A. (2015). Developing the 3 habits of transformational leaders. Forbes, August 27, 2015. Retrieved from http://www.forbes.com/sites/yec/2015/08/27/developing-the-3-habits-of-transformational-leaders/#ca3aec11c45b

APPENDIX

Books

Aronoff, C. E., & Baskin, O. W. (2011). *Effective leadership in the family business.* New York, NY: Palgrave Macmillan US.

Aronoff, C. E., & Ward, J. L. (2011). *Family business governance: Maximizing family and business potential.* New York, NY: Palgrave Macmillan US.

Aronoff, C. E., & Ward, J. L. (2011). *Family business ownership: How to be an effective shareholder.* New York, NY: Palgrave Macmillan US.

Aronoff, C. E., & Ward, J. L. (2011). *Family business values: How to assure a legacy of continuity and success.* New York, NY: Palgrave Macmillan US.

Aronoff, C. E., & Ward, J. L. (2011). *From siblings to cousins: Prospering in the third generation and beyond.* New York, NY: Palgrave Macmillan US.

Carlock, R. S., & Ward, J. L. (2010). When family businesses are best: The parallel planning process for family harmony and business success. New York, NY: Palgrave Macmillan US.

Eckrich, C. J., & McClure, S. L. (2012). *The family council handbook.* New York, NY: Palgrave Macmillan US.

Gersick, K. E., Davis, J. A., Hampton, M. M., & Lansberg, I. (1997). *Generation to generation.* Boston, MA: Harvard Business School.

Goleman, D. (1995). *Emotional intelligence.* New York, NY: Bantam.

Hughes, J., Massenzio, S.E., & Whitaker, K. (2014), *Voice of the rising generation.* Hoboken, NJ: Wiley.

Jaffe, D.T. (2010). *Stewardship in your family enterprise.* Charleston, SC: Pioneer Imprints.

Jaffe, D.T. (2013). Good fortune: Building a hundred year family enterprise. Milton, MA: Wise Counsel Research.

Lansky, D. (2016). Family wealth continuity: Building a foundation for the future. New York, NY: Palgrave MacMillan US.

Miller, D.,& Miller, I.L. (2005). Managing for the long run: Lessons in competitive advantage from great family businesses. Boston, MA: Harvard Business School Press.

Schuman, A., Stutz, S., & Ward, J.L. (2010). *Family business as paradox.* New York, NY: Palgrave Macmillan US.

Schuman, A., & Ward, J.L. (2011). Family education for business-owning families: Strengthening bonds by learning together. New York, NY: Palgrave Macmillan US.

Peter Senge (2005). The fifth discipline: The art and practice of the learning organization. New York, NY: Doubleday.

Family Business Centers

Many universities and colleges have family business centers with educational programming and speakers. Check with your local institutions to see if they have these resources. Here are some prominent programs:

- Loyola University (Chicago, IL): Quinlan School of Business, Family Business Center.
  http://www.luc.edu/quinlan/fbc/

- St. Joseph's University (Philadelphia, PA): The Initiative for Family Business and Entrepreneurship.
  http://sites.sju.edu/ifbe/

- University of Wisconsin (Madison, WI): Wisconsin School of Business, Family Business Center. http://uwfbc.org/

- Centenary College (Shreveport, LA): Frost School of Business, Center for Family-Owned Business (CFOB).
  https://www.centenary.edu/academics/departments-schools/frost-school-of-business/community-commitment/center-for-family-owned-business/

APPENDIX

- University of British Columbia (Vancouver BC, Canada): UBC Sauder School of Business, Business Families Centre (BFC). http://www.sauder.ubc.ca/Programs/Business_Families _Centre

- Saginaw Valley State University (University Center, MI): SVSU College of Business and Management. The Stevens Center for Family Business (SCFB). http://www.svsu.edu/stevenscenterforfamilybusiness/

ABOUT THE AUTHORS

Joshua Nacht is actively involved in two separate family businesses: one that his father started (a real estate business in the Vail Valley) and one that he married into (Bird). Josh served on the family council and as a family representative on the board of directors of Bird, a 75-year-old business based in Cleveland, Ohio, that builds radio frequency power measurement components and systems.

After completing his bachelor's degree in English Literature from Cornell College in Iowa and a master's in counseling from Naropa University in Colorado, Josh became interested in organizational behavior and was inspired by family business professor and advisor John Ward to pursue his doctorate in family enterprise.

Josh completed his PhD at Saybrook University in 2015 under the guidance of visionary family business expert Dennis Jaffe. He joined The Family Business Consulting Group in 2015, working as a consultant with a variety of business families, seeing the dynamics of family champions and champion families firsthand.

Greg Greenleaf is a Principal Consultant with The Family Business Consulting Group. Prior to becoming an advisor to enterprising families, Greg worked in both of his family businesses, first as a machinist at Greenleaf Corporation, a manufacturer of industrial cutting tools in Northwestern Pennsylvania, and later as a Sales Engineer, and ultimately as President of the Walter J. Greenleaf Company, a regional industrial distribution and manufacturer's representative organization founded by his grandfather.

Previously, Greg completed his master's degree in Counseling Psychology at Lesley University in Massachusetts and worked as a counselor to individuals, couples, and families before returning to the family business.

Greg began advising family businesses as a mentor with the Institute of Entrepreneurial Excellence at the University of Pittsburgh. With the encouragement of other family business leaders, Greg realized that his deep knowledge and experience managing a complex family business, combined with his psychology training and counseling experience, provided him with a valuable set of tools to guide other family businesses facing wide-ranging challenges. Greg began advising family firms part-time, finding genuine passion for the work. He joined The Family Business Consulting Group in 2005 and became a Principal Consultant in 2012.

INDEX

Manufactured by Amazon.ca
Bolton, ON

23503190R00087